NEW WELSH READER

FATHERS AND DAUGHTERS

New Welsh Reader
New Welsh Review Ltd
PO Box 170, Aberystwyth, SY23 1WZ
Telephone: 01970 628410
www.newwelshreview.com

Editor:
Gwen Davies
editor@newwelshreview.com

Administration & Finance Officer:
Bronwen Williams
admin@newwelshreview.com

Marketing & Publicity Officer:
Jemma Bezant
marketing@newwelshreview.com

Management Board:
Ali Anwar, Gwen Davies (Director),
Andrew Green (Director, Chair), Ruth
Killick, David Michael (Treasurer),
Matthew Francis, Emily Blewitt (Poetry
Submissions Editor, Vice-Chair).

Poetry Submissions Filter:
Gwen Davies

**Sponsor of the New Welsh Writing
Awards:** RS Powell

Design: Ingleby Davies Design

Main images: Cover: 'RS Thomas, Kyffin
Williams and Emyr Humphreys, 1999',
© MR Thomas. Contents: (top) Swill
Klitch / Shutterstock, (right) Suzy
Hazelwood / Pexels.

Host: Aberystwyth University

The New Welsh Review Ltd publishes with
the financial support of the Books Council
of Wales, and is hosted by Aberystwyth
University's Department of English &
Creative Writing. The New Welsh Review
Ltd was established in 1988 by Academi
(now Literature Wales) and the Association
for Welsh Writing in English. *New Welsh
Reader* is New Welsh Review's print (and
digital) magazine for creative work. We
also publish monthly roundups of online
content, including reviews, comment and
poetry, and at least one book annually on
the New Welsh Rarebyte imprint, run a
writing competition (New Welsh Writing
Awards), and improve diversity in the UK
publishing industry by hosting student
work placements.

Mae croeso ichi ohebu â'r golygydd
yn Gymraeg.

Patrons: Belinda Humfrey, Owen Sheers

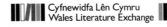

SIGN UP!

Our new website can be browsed by category, theme tag or title and is now a one-stop shop for our ePub formats and fully searchable digital archive, books, offers and more. New-look digital editions are fully searchable, have a page-turning feature and include complete text-to-speech (TTS) element as standard..

NEW WELSH REVIEW REVIEWS, COMMENT, MULTIMEDIA

Elaine Morgan: A Life Behind the Screen Daryl Leeworthy (Seren). Sarah Broughton on how the screen- and science-writer's modest persona shielded astonishing success and lifelong themes of inequality, feminism and left-wing politics

Echoes from a Small Country Katie Gramich remembers Siân James, noting how, in her fiction, class and gender intermingle and exacerbate the oppression in women's lives

The End of the Yellow House Alan Bilton (Watermark). Michael Stein on how this surreal and comic novel upends all rules of the mystery, merging it with history, horror and Russian literary art

Flashbacks and Flowers Rufus Mufasa (Indigo Dreams). Natalia Elliot on a poetry collection about transgenerational trauma and motherhood (audio review with subtitles and digital storytelling)

JULES WILLIAMS

Rufus Mufasa

NEW WELSH READER 129 ESSAYS, MEMOIR, STORIES, POETRY

'The Broken Mountain' Second in Steven Lovatt's travel writing series from 'Notes from a Hungarian Journal'

'Tidelands' First in a new series by Angela Evans on Wales' unsung estuary landscapes, with photographs by David Street

'Hearth' Story by Jem Poster

Kyffin Williams, RS Thomas and Emyr Humphreys, 1999.
© MR THOMAS

THE PENTREFELIN THREE

MR THOMAS ON THE OCTOBER DAY IN 1999 WHEN HE SHOT
THE GROUP PORTRAIT OF CULTURAL ICONS RS THOMAS,
KYFFIN WILLIAMS AND EMYR HUMPHREYS

Friday 1 October, 1999

ON A MORNING OF CALIGINOUS GLOOM, AND IN A STATE OF SOME AGITATION, I hastened south across Eifionydd, bound for the home of the poet. Even by his own reckoning, RS Thomas was said to be on his last legs, and certain to be much changed from the bard I'd seen blowing in from the night to recite his poems in Bangor Cathedral three years before. Ahead of me now, the road was a pearly line streaked across dismal fields studded with hawthorn thickets and lustrous beasts. An empty school bus bowled past. Rain speckled the windscreen. Huddled in the back were the other men I was gathering this day: Kyffin Williams, muffled up in the rustic colours of his palette, was regaling the novelist Emyr Humphreys with a well-polished yarn. Their friendship stretched back fifty years to the confines of Griffs Bookshop, then a haven for those Welshmen and Welshwomen marooned in post-war London. I caught snatches of conversation. 'Your moustache was red then,' I heard Emyr say.

Wiping moisture from the window, Kyffin looked out onto the purpling fissile upland of Maes Tryfan that he had drawn so often. He began to ponder the poet's recent return to Pen Llŷn. 'You see, I'm certainly *not* a Welsh nationalist,' he stressed, 'but I know Welsh nats who live around here and he won't have anything to do with them.' Wind buffeted the car. More's the pity, Kyffin went on, how the public always seemed to get the wrong impression of RS. 'It's as though he's just some monstrous old curmudgeon.'

'Well, there we are,' sighed Emyr, 'people have *always* thought of him as part of the rock, but *we* know he's not like that.' I caught his hesitant blue eyes in the mirror. 'Anyway, what do you have in mind for *us*, then?'

I looked back to the road. How to put it? My intentions had been assured over the phone, to unite three men of an age who had seen their country transformed, and given us – through poetry, painting and prose – their vision of Wales and the Welsh.

But now I dithered and garbled a reply. 'I may have had *A Toy Epic* in mind,' I added rashly, referring to Emyr's celebrated novella about three boys from different corners of north Wales whose lives touch and cross as they grow old. I glanced up again but the men had resumed their conversation. At Bryncir, we turned off onto a back road which curled and dipped towards the sea. For the last few miles we tailed a cattle truck spilling clods.

In Pentrefelin, the poet's cottage lay fast against the old droveway beneath the broad bare boughs of an ash. Twll y Cae had once stood at 'the gap in the copse' between four mills, but now it nestled between a pebbledash bungalow and the curious Goat Villa. Slates had long replaced straw, but roughcast brick beneath blinding whitewash still evoked a distant past. A spiral of amber leaves spun in the yard, and from the open door came a loudening giggle. It was Mrs Thomas, more stooped and toothy than before, but just as sassy, her eyes twinkling from deep, emerald shadows.

'Ah Betty!' beamed Kyffin, doffing his cap.

'Well hello to the men,' she gabbled in her Canadian drawl. 'Ronnie boy won't be long. He's just with the nurse.'

She beckoned us in. The porch gave onto a narrow tiled passage, off which lay intimate rooms dotted with chinoiserie and bird figurines. Betty halted at the entrance to the lounge. The carpet was strewn with buckets.

'Huh!' she snapped. 'Bloody rain came in last night! We're besieged with bloody damp, so you'll have to go in here.' She ushered us into an adjacent room, which was as dim and dank as a vestry. At its centre was a small round table with four chairs. 'Kettle's on,' she called back.

We stood about, expectant. A door closed. Footsteps.

'Wel, dyma ni.'

There was dust on his shoulders and – framed in the backlight – his spindrift hair seemed like a cascade of firework trails. He loured at us – professionally, you might say – and then pulled the most malevolent grin. RS Thomas seemed content with his new congregation. The three shook hands, awkward laughter began to swirl the room, and I excused myself to help Betty in the kitchen. She was placing biscuits on a plate and pouring herself an emergency brandy.

'Smoke anything I can get my hands on,' she muttered, swilling the pot. I declined a cigarette and asked her about the house.

'Used to be an inn,' she said. Ash fell onto a biscuit. 'Clough did it over.' She brushed it off. 'This and the old parsonage.' She told me it was the first home they'd owned, but that most of the chattels were hers. 'The accumulation of various marriages,' she said with a wink.

I noticed, above the kettle, a framed piece of notepaper with a few scrawled lines in the poet's hand. She saw me smile and jabbed me with her elbow. 'People have him all bloody wrong,' she giggled. I read it out.

RST TIMETABLE

Get up. Wash. Shave.
Get Betty's and my breakfast.
Sit in study. Read. Sleep.
Lunch. Sit. End up asleep.
Tea. News. Doze before supper.
Watch TV. Supper. Prepare for bed.

When I rejoined the three, they were circling the 1920s. I began to take notes. With a nervous chuckle, Emyr was pointing out Sir John Morris-Jones' 'very fine translation' of Omar Khayyam into Welsh. 'At another point in time,' he went on fervently, 'Morris-Jones had dared to make fun of the Gorsedd, saying it had no antiquity and was all made up by Iolo Morganwg. A reviewer, I think by the name of T Marchant Williams, led the retaliation by describing Sir John's book of poems *Caniadau* as "machine-made poetry on handmade paper".'

Kyffin Williams, Emyr Humphreys and RS Thomas, 1999 (pencil on paper).
© MR THOMAS

'Ha!' cried Kyffin, throwing his head back and folding his arms in his sleeves. I noticed the buttoning of his cardigan was awry.

RS passed a shaky finger across his lower lip. 'Well, it's a bit like the Eisteddfod itself,' he said, resignedly. 'It's a pity it ever reached the state it has, because it was a good idea originally to push the poets together to try and formalise their craft. Then it ran wild.' The voice tremored with age. His jacket fell away from his chest and he scraped his thumbs along sharp red braces.

At the recent Eisteddfod in Llanbedr-goch he had admitted to finding little or no pleasure in the poetry of the young and had appealed to the National Assembly to support English-medium writers. He hoped they would acknowledge literature as one of Wales' greatest gifts, because it was through literature, he stressed, that a nation becomes conscious of itself.

Talk of the Eisteddfod drew Kyffin up in his seat. 'It's oft been hijacked,' he said peevishly. 'The Eisteddfod has the largest private audience in the country, but the ordinary Welsh folk who go there just get smitten between their ears! They are not served by the Arts Council. All they have is this modern junk hammered at them....' He checked himself and lowered his fist, no doubt realising he was preaching to the converted. A hush fell upon the party and the room seemed at once deeply private as the three leant in on pinched chins, like a council of Druids convening in secret.

RS retreated to the Middle Ages. 'So what's happening to Llew's old tŵr at Aber?' he enquired openly, mentioning the last sovereign Prince of Wales as if he were an old friend.

Kyffin shrugged unknowingly but then announced how pleased he was that at long last a commemorative plaque to William Jones had been erected on Anglesey.

'William Jones?' echoed Emyr. He searched for a connection. 'Ah yes, the mathematician. A very important man. The father of William Jones India, or "Oriental Jones", as they used to call him. The man who rediscovered Sanskrit, no less.'

Emyr's erudition was as impressive as ever, but in this instance I sensed an over-eagerness to display it, as if to induce RS into conversation. He looked to him often, with a certain quizzical reverence that brought to mind a moment at Emyr's house when he had pulled from his bookcase a copy of RS' first collection, *The Stones of the Field*, given to him by the poet. I could still picture him, delicately opening the cover to show me the playful inscription inside. *From an unwise poet,* it read, *to an even more unwise novelist.*

I asked about their first encounter.

'We were taken up by Keidrych Rhys,' replied Emyr. 'That's how we met.'

'No no,' insisted RS, 'we were taken *in* by him....'

It was the summer of 1946, and Keidrych Rhys, the editor of the literary journal *Wales*, was up from his home in Carmarthenshire and had persuaded RS to drive them both in his first wife's car on a tour of his contributors.

Emyr was one of them. 'It was outside Bodfach Hall near Llanfyllin,' he explained, 'where I was working as a youth organiser, for my sins. And my first sight of you, Ronald, was of you and Keidrych climbing out of Elsi's Austin Seven. It was as if you were breaking from an eggshell.'

RS shed a smile. 'Keidrych was a good editor,' he replied, tapping his finger on the table and shooting Emyr a sidelong glance, 'about *all* you could say for him, though.'

'Pffh, well,' Emyr pulled a face, 'he *was* a significant figure.'

RS conceded a nod. It was Keidrych, after all, who had published his first collection.

'In fact, I had the very first issue of *Wales*,' said Emyr, still keen to give Keidrych his due. 'I was still at school, and I can remember vividly that it had Dylan on the cover, *As I walked through the wilderness of this world....*'

Keidrych's journal had been a conscious attempt to give voice to 'younger progressive Welsh writers' like RS and Emyr, who would come to favour *Wales* over Gwyn Jones' rival journal *Welsh Review*, for its respect to the writer and political activist Saunders Lewis, who was, to the young poet and novelist, the key figure in the nation's life and literature.

'We firmly believed,' Emyr maintained, 'that a close attention to Saunders' message was the best hope for a Welsh future.'

Betty rattled in with the Portmeirion. Emyr urged her to join us but she was still fussing over the floodstains, and scurried out. We took tea, and as we did so the room began to darken and there came a sudden fall of leaves past the small panes of the low set window. The men closed in under a single lamp. Their hair formed a white glow. Then a peal of thunder brought a searing thought: this gathering, these three huddled into a corner of Wales in the dying days of their century, would never recur. The room would soon be a vacuum. I put my pen aside and sat back to absorb the tableau, with all the wonder of the uninitiated. Kyffin slouched in his chair and pressed his thumbs together, poised to rattle off untold tales. Beside him, Emyr remained pensive, though furtive looks habitually gave way to aphorism. 'The outside world is a reflection of what's inside us,' he said now, perhaps to prompt RS, whose utterances alternated between dry witticisms and sour finalities. It was hard to take your eye off the poet. Still there came that unsparing gaze, but around it now were deeper implosions and sinuous lines. I watched as he drew in his lips to take another sup of tea, and was transfixed by the machinery of bone and musculature, like cogs winding down. A face at journey's end.

The clouds passed, the room brightened and I caught the last threads of them ruminating on regional dialects and a woman down south who taught recitation and sang carols whilst mimicking a turkey gobble. Emyr then drew us back to the Eisteddfod, to talk of ovates and bards and of a former Archdruid James Nicholas.

'Funny, isn't it, the trend of language,' said RS. 'I mean, the Welsh for James is Iago. How did he become Jâms? Jâms, eh? Why couldn't he have been Iago Niclas? There's something phoney about it....' He trailed off, privately aggrieved.

'And yet,' said the silent listener in the corner, 'certain nice things happen in the language. If you want to ring someone you can give them a *caniad*, and so a pleasant call can "sing" to you.'

'Better than teleffonio,' quipped RS with a puckish curl to his lip.

Kyffin suddenly broke in with gusto. 'When I was in Patagonia,' he announced, 'there was a law decreeing that no Argentinian child could be christened with a Welsh name. But they got around this. Not only were there many Ricardos, Robertos and even Evanos but I once stayed in a house where there was a little boy christened Diego... but known as Iago.' He capped his anecdote with another. 'They were wonderfully inventive. When the first aeroplane flew over the valley, a newborn girl was christened Aviona, and with the arrival of electricity, another was called Aluminada.'

It was more than thirty years since Kyffin had visited that distant Welsh colony, and yet his eyes still glistened at the mention of it. 'Ah, they were all so nice,' he said to Emyr through a satisfied smile. 'I'm still there, you know.' And he talked about the vast yellow desert and how he had planned to ride across it, and the warnings, and the old bus. 'I made seven hundred drawings altogether, and when I got back I thought it would be foolish to sell my record so I offered them to the National Museum of Wales, but they gave me a bloody nose!'

'How do you mean?' asked Emyr.

'They told me to get lost. So I offered them to the National Library and they took them, which was very lucky because if the Museum had said yes, they would have thrown them in the basement, never to be seen again, but because of the National Library, they've been going around Wales in exhibitions ever since.'

RS narrowed his eyes at Kyffin. 'Did you encounter much *English*?' he asked with characteristic disdain for that idiom. 'Were they able to speak *English*, the people you met?'

'Not many, no.'

'And had any of them known Wales?'

'Ah well, now, there was a man called Glyn Ceiriog Hughes who acted as my guide, and he said that when his father returned from visiting Wales for the only time, they had all waited eagerly to hear what the old country was like. "Wales?" said Glyn Ceiriog's father, "Well, it was a funny little place. Everywhere I went I was knocking my nose!"'

For all their tweed and twill and refined cadence, you'd have thought that RS and Kyffin were old muckers, and indeed they could have been if only their cricket fixtures – they played for Holyhead and Porthmadog when young – had ever coincided. But their formal introduction had only come in recent years, when the painter had gone to sketch the poet for a portrait. And during these encounters, they talked not of poems or paintings, but of birds and their solitary boyhoods. Young Ronald had roamed Anglesey's coast to watch for sea fowl, young Kyffin to watch the waves, and with their fathers often away, both had been at the spoil and mercy of domineering matriarchs. 'It's a funny thing, you know, but old RS and I had very similar mothers,' Kyffin had told me on another occasion, 'both Anglophile and Cymruphobic.' Kyffin's mother had declared Wales a vulgar nation and banned Welsh at home. 'I was brainwashed against it," he said. Likewise, RS had been denied the language in his youth, and would later memorably describe how he'd sucked in English with his mother's 'infected milk'. As a boy, Emyr too had been held back from learning Welsh by a father who deemed it an unnecessary hindrance to middle-class aspirations. The three had reclaimed their birthright ever since.

The conversation turned to a recent article in the *Daily Post*. The pious folk of one valley had called a meeting to discuss their minister's conduct, even debating his earring, but before they could reach a consensus, he'd run off with a girl from Abersoch. The new incumbent was a woman.

'A vicarette....' said RS.

'You can't open the papers these days,' grumbled Emyr, 'without some bishop or other....'

RS cut in with a heavy sigh. 'I just loathe it all,' he said, his voice faltering. 'It was poor old Bonhoeffer who started all this. Publicly such a good man, but this "religionless Christianity". The whole ablution....' He stopped short, perhaps unwilling to declaim how his own poetry had tended to deride that lunatic fringe who believe in a godless faith. 'It's bringing into the open what a lot of people think,' he added with a slight scoff of derision. 'You know, that I don't need to go to a chapel or a church to be good.' He paused again, for longer this time, before muttering under his breath, 'You're much safer with the birds to God.'

Now there was a line for a poem. Or a priest's confession? How apposite, I thought, that above his bowed head hung a framed red kite feather, a memento from the days when there was but a single breeding pair left in Wales. *Safer with the birds to God*. His words hung between us, until – without response – they dissolved ever so slowly into the reaches of the room.

My mind drifted. 'I don't know *what* sort of Christian he is,' I recalled Kyffin once saying as he puzzled over the poet's faith, 'but then God is really the bird of nature.'

RS wrestled an apophatic theology. God was notable by his great absence, as elusive as those red kites, but the divine could always be sought in nature. *He is in the flowers,* so he had once written, *and in the white water, and in the throat of a bird.*

RS drew his thumb and forefinger together at his neck. 'What amuses me,' he said with a slow oscillation of his head, 'is how the band of white cloth has gradually shrunk over the years.'

Kyffin chipped in, telling us how his taid, when rector of Llanrhuddlad, had always refused to wear a dog-collar unless it was official business, instead sporting a white paper bow-tie which had to be made each morning by one of his many sons.

'The width of the collar,' continued RS, undeterred by the eccentric aside, 'once depended on the highness or lowness of your churchmanship. At one period if you were a "spike", as they called Anglo-Catholics, you had a very narrow strip which gradually widened to one of these really tall ones that denoted you were a high churcher.' He went on, without looking up, 'I tried to find out from somebody what the difference was between Monsignor and Monseigneur, and the answer came that there was no real difference at all, only in their mind. Emyr, you remember Bruce Kent, the CND chap. He was a Monsignor.' RS cleared his throat and splayed his fingers on the tablecloth. There was more on his mind. 'You know, when I was campaigning with CND, I used to say, 'We *are* right, and whatever the other side says, we *are* right. And it is there you know, isn't it?'

Emyr was quick to concur. It was the poet's unyielding stance and the sight of his stern figure outside power plants and law courts, his hair in the wind, that had led Emyr to hail RS a prophetic figure. *Let it be understood, poets are dangerous,* Emyr had written recently in honour of his old friend, *they undermine the state; they thrust before congregations hymns they would prefer not to hear.*

RS was still pondering the cause. 'Remember that awful man Marshall,' he continued, 'who used to go around saying, "Three things about nuclear power: It's safe, it's clean, and it's cheap." Three lies, *three lies,* and he was made a peer.'

There was silence, and tacit glances between us. Despite the frailty, there was vim in the old poet yet. Emyr straightened his cuffs.

'You sometimes expect these people to reappear,' he replied quietly, 'like ghosts on television. Talking of which, there was a very nasty programme on last night about Goronwy Rees.'

Kyffin raised his eyebrows at this. 'Old Goronwy loved to flirt with danger,' he said, 'but I've always been certain he was no traitor. There he was on the periphery, but I don't think he ever jumped in.'

The BBC Wales documentary to which Emyr referred had come in the wake of new allegations of espionage by KGB defector Vasili Mitrohkin. Emyr had known Goronwy in the years after he had left Aberystwyth under a cloud. 'A good writer,' he surmised, 'but a dangerous chap.' Rees' onslaught against Welsh culture and his articles about his friend, the Soviet defector Guy Burgess, had not only cost him his job as principal of the university but had also pitted the Welsh intelligentsia against him. 'I can well remember,' Emyr recalled, 'when I was working as a producer for the BBC in London alongside people like Louis MacNeice and Terence Tiller, that there was a feeling Goronwy had been unfairly treated by these stuffy Welsh philistines.'

RS had remained silent on the topic, but a name pulled him back into the conversation. 'MacNeice was the best of that lot, to my mind,' he said, his eyes darting between us as if expecting a challenge that did not come. 'I don't accept this lionisation of Auden. I think he is over rated [he split the word purposefully]. A sacred tower of academia, about which you mustn't say anything disagreeable.' He acknowledged Auden as a craftsman but one with little value or depth. 'I can recall how, if you were to speak in certain company, they'd turn on you and say, "Ah yes, but Auden. He was a *great* poet." But they don't say *why*, and quote from his work to bolster what they're saying. And, you know, as Goebbels said, if you repeat something often enough, people will start to believe it.'

'Another biscuit?' I asked, pushing the plate forward.

RS raised a declining hand. 'As you like,' he mumbled.

Kyffin clattered his cup in its saucer. 'That's always happened in art too,' he said, 'when someone is picked up and raised to sanctity, and nothing can trip them.'

'Elsi and I were once visiting the Tate,' RS began again, 'where the director, John Rothenstein, was showing two or three people around. They stopped in front of Graham Sutherland's portrait of Somerset Maugham, and Rothenstein – turning to his group – said, 'Now that's a *very* good Sutherland.' Well, it was nothing to do with me but I wanted him to expand and say *why*, because I don't know enough about painting. It needs to be asked more often, as with Auden.'

The books lining the walls of the cottage, remnants from the poet's peregrinations, were a testament to his long interest in art, much of it imbued from his first wife Elsi, a highly gifted illustrator and muralist. There were volumes on Russian painting, on Blake, Monet, Iznik pottery, David Jones, Vermeer, Zurbarán, Tunnicliffe and Byzantium, and even a book I'd sent him on Christian pictures and their meanings.

'The trouble with living out in the bush as I have done,' said RS after a lengthy pause, 'is that I've had to rely on reproductions for most of my knowledge of art. I did some pastiches based on paintings in the Louvre but they were far from the real thing.'

Kyffin pushed back his heavy forelock and smoothed the tips of his moustaches. He began to explain how Graham Sutherland had long been considered the only painter to convey Pembrokeshire. 'But I believe he pre-imagined it in his studio before he ever went there.' In his view, Sutherland wasn't an emotional artist but a clinical one. He accepted that his ideas and their execution joined in a contemporary manner but that they didn't translate the land. 'I don't believe he ever saw a horizon. Pembrokeshire is full of them, but he was looking at his feet.'

Emyr knew that landscape intimately. As a conscientious objector, he had worked on farms there during the war, and said he couldn't reconcile its colours with Sutherland's palette.

'He concocted the colour. It's never natural. It came from here,' Kyffin tapped his forehead. 'I am not a colourist, but I try and get the tones right, and I *assist* my colour and if you assist your colours, nothing needeth go wrong.'

RS stared up at the brass-framed landscape by Kyffin which loomed over us from above the mantelpiece. Devoid of views from his thick-walled tyddyn bach, the painting of a still grey Gwynant, ringed by lime green shores and mussel-blue peaks, gave the poet a window on his world. 'But I mean Kyffin, spare his blushes,' he said, his frown lifting. 'Kyffin *conveys* Wales in a way that Sutherland never *conveyed* Pembrokeshire.'

Kyffin took the compliment bashfully. 'Well, I'm lucky, I'm a local boy,' he said by way of an explanation. 'I suppose it's given me an advantage.'

'I mean, at least there's something *there*,' said RS, motioning at the painting. 'What could you say about Sutherland? How much was there *there*? Those horrid little bits of prickly gorse on a wall. Hmm... perhaps I'm doing him an injustice. I ought to have seen a lot more Sutherlands before I venture to speak. Which side of Moel Hebog were you, Kyffin?'

'That's looking onto the lake from half way down Snowdon on the slopes of Moel Meirch.'

With a wistful groan, RS told us there was a twll up there he had not seen. And he would never see it now, for he no longer had the strength to climb another mountain, nor so, he claimed, the concentration to compose another poem. A year back he had let it be known that there would be no successor to his previous volume, *No Truce with the Furies,* and besides, he was now of the opinion that the new generation of poets saw right through him.

Kyffin turned and looked his painting over for a moment. 'I was hoping to keep it for an exhibition,' he said. Then leaning towards me, his voice dropping to an audible whisper, 'You see, I don't usually sell from the studio... but Betty was insistent.'

'I heard that!' she hollered from the other room.

I could see that RS was retreating again to autumn thoughts, so I suggested we move outside, to catch the last light for a photograph. Whilst gathering my things, I happened to place on the table my old Pelican paperback copy of *The Welsh* by Llewelyn Wyn Griffith, a book I often referred to. RS reached across for it, saying how much he had admired Wyn's short stories in *Y Fflam*. One of them was entitled 'Y Dyn Diarth' (The Godless Man). It was in that same periodical that RS had penned some of his own first writings in Welsh.

'I liked old Wyn,' said Kyffin, to murmurs of agreement. He had painted his portrait during the 1950s, and he divulged to us how, during that sitting, Wyn had recounted his harrowing experience as a Royal Welsh Fusilier during the Great War. 'Well you see, Wyn was commanding a company in Mametz Wood,' explained Kyffin, settling back, 'and he'd already sent two runners to the front with messages, in an attempt to stop the field artillery from shelling their own men. But both had been killed, and so a third runner was sent, none other than Wyn's younger brother, Watcyn. He delivered his message but was killed on the way back. Wyn, I think, knew that he'd sent him to his death, and this is why he wrote *Up To Mametz*.'

'A profile man,' said RS, turning the book over in his hands and pointing out the author's picture on the reverse. 'He was often photographed from the side.' And with that, he rose from his seat and led us to the back door.

The wind soughed in the hedgerow rustling the shrubbery and bending the tips of the Irish yews. In each lull, one could hear the babble of a brook which ran past the edge of the garden and under the road. I put out three wooden slatted chairs.

'The Penyberth Three', Lewis Valentine, Saunders Lewis and DJ Williams.
IN PUBLIC DOMAIN

'Are they dry?' RS asked me with a roguish grin, 'because if we get piles it will be impossible to prove that it was *this* that caused it.'

They sat and talked a while longer. RS and Emyr bantered in Welsh. I hovered over them with my old Pentax, then asked that they stand up against a blank wall of the cottage.

'It'll be like that one of Saunders, Valentine and DJ,' said RS.

Exactly that, I silently hoped.

'Yes indeed, the Penyberth Three,' Emyr concurred. 'Amazing how that photograph of them became an icon. It was virtually accidental you know.'

The arson attack on the RAF base at Penyberth in 1936 by Plaid Cymru members Saunders Lewis, DJ Williams and Lewis Valentine had been to the seventeen-year-old Emyr Humphreys a blazing reassertion of national identity. It converted him into a nationalist before he'd even grasped the language. He must have still been mulling over the photograph of the three arsonists for he suddenly offered up a line from *Twelfth Night*. 'Did you never see the picture of "we three"?' he said to RS with a certain glee.

Typically, Kyffin had an anecdote at the ready. 'Old Saunders wrote to me once,' he said enticingly, 'saying he wanted to meet up, and would I come to the Farmers' Club off Whitehall on a certain day at a certain time. So I put on a suit and went along with Ceri Richards, and I was introduced to this wizened little man who looked up at me with those great wet orbs and said, "Duw, I don't believe it!" The *only* words he would *ever* say to me. You see, I'd no Welsh, no tatty corduroys, no boots stuck with dung.'

After the laughing, I asked them to vary their stance. RS locked his fingers behind his back and puffed out his chest, Emyr plunged his hands into his pockets and frowned, Kyffin folded his arms and cocked his head.

'And you've not been photographed together before?' I asked.

'No,' said RS, smiling at the others and then at me, 'this is why the fee is so high....'

MR Thomas is an award-winning documentary filmmaker, formerly for BBC Arts and now freelance. For the past thirty years, he has been interviewing and photographing the writers and artists of Wales. His photographs have appeared in *The Guardian*, *The Times*, *The Herald*, *Radio Times* and *Agenda*. An iconic press photograph (pictured) of 'The Penyberth Three' – Lewis Valentine, Saunders Lewis and DJ Williams – taken in 1936, prompted him to unite RS Thomas, Kyffin Williams and Emyr Humphreys for a similar group portrait in October 1999 at the poet's home in Pentrefelin, just over ten miles from Penyberth.

THE BROKEN MOUNTAIN

THE FIRST PART IN A NEW SERIES
OF TRAVEL WRITING BY **STEVEN LOVATT**,
'NOTES FROM A HUNGARIAN JOURNAL'

HALÁP IS A BROKEN MOUNTAIN, AND THERE IS LITTLE MORE MELANCHOLY than that. Halfway up the southern slope, frowning slightly under thick wooden gables, among yellowing lanes of vineyards and fruit trees, Géza and Rita have a house around which lean cats slouch on lazy orbits, attracted by the fragrant steam from the chicken soup that's sieved out through the mosquito netting. While Rita sees to the soup, Géza chops logs with his hornbeam-hafted axe or plays endless games of patience on his computer, beneath a map of Hungary as it was before the Treaty of Trianon. On the next storey there is a terrace whose bitumen awning has been punctured by the same freakish late summer hailstones that pocked the violet plums and panicked the vintners between here and Keszthely. And it is from this terrace that one can see the other mountains, the unbroken ones: Csobánc, Kistőti, Nemes-Gulács, Badacsony and Szent-György.

All of the mountains around here are volcanic, but only Haláp has a crater, blasted not by magma but by dynamite driven gingerly up the uneven stony track in lorries on hire to basalt extractors. Géza and Rita seem proud that the paving stones of Budapest, London and Paris contain basalt from Haláp, but it is a desolate thing at dusk to stand in the centre of that grasshopper-plagued crater, surrounded by the severed hexagons of basalt and the stone rubble from the blasting. No trees grow here, but there are snakes in the scrub, and eagles sometimes drift this way when a south wind nuzzles the hill and sets the updraughts rising.

...

On the second evening we drove back from the lake where the children had spent the day playing on floats and poking their toes into the thick grey silt in search of freshwater mussels. The café played Eddie Cochrane and served over-salted trout, and *langos* with soured cream and red onions. A family was talking politics, switching between Hungarian and German. The lady said that every day hundreds of Syrians are still crossing from Hungary, via Austria, into Germany; but her son, his authority enhanced by the Dynamo Dresden beach towel around his waist, insisted that the German border is now closed. Later, while everyone was busy, I took the dinghy and the marigold paddle out beyond the part-submerged volleyball goals and even the furthest swimmers to the reed-beds where I lay quietly to watch the warblers that flit and scrape there in the swaying shade, clinging to the reeds like notation on vertical staves. There is such peace to be had in those gullies of green water, where the beach noise doesn't carry and the only sound is the whisper of the reeds and the sudden dither of moorhens disturbed by the bungling dinghy from their nests in the sedge.

As we drove up to the house on the hill towards nightfall we saw another car on the orchard grass. Rita told me that it was owned by the *palinka* man, a licensed distiller of the national spirit, who can be summoned at short notice by the local fruit producers and will then return two weeks later with plastic bottles containing alcohol infused with apricot, cherry or just about anything. But Julia said that when she had overheard Géza arranging the visit on the previous day, the conversation had taken place in an obscure argot and thick accents of conspiracy, 'So maybe he doesn't have a license after all.' As the sun winked out behind Haláp, draining the translucency from the under-skins of the small red plums, the *palinka* man grinned at us shyly from under an enormous black moustache and then rattled off down the gravel track, the back seat jittery with white tubs of fruit.

* * *

'What is Slovakia!' We have just finished our meal in the house on the hill. The children only picked at their food and then ran, pursued by futile remonstrations, back out into the garden where they are building palaces in the sandpit for their toy ponies. But it is better that they are not here to witness Géza in full flow. He is leaning back in his chair, but his face is animated. He fixes me with eyes pink around the lids: 'How old is Slovakia? My belt is older! How many kings have the Slovakians had?' The room suddenly seems very small. It doesn't matter that nobody answers Géza's questions, because we all know he will answer them himself. Back home in England, our Slovakian friend Zuzana minds the children regularly to allow us some time out, and is helping me with some translations of the Slovakian poet Maša Haľamová.

Géza is of a type that does not exist in Britain. Orphaned early, he was raised by his grandparents on a remote Transylvanian mountainside, where he guarded the horses and each October watched his grandfather slit the throat of the winter pig. When he descended to the valley in order to go to school, he was viciously bullied by his Romanian-speaking classmates. Later he was drafted into the Romanian army and endured more of the same treatment during the two years he spent in a barracks on the Black Sea coast. By this time, however, he had learned how to fight. After completing his service he fled Romania with his broth-ers, and settled in a border town in the east of Hungary. He married and had children. His son was eighteen when he was approached by a local criminal who threatened him with death if he did not help a gang to smuggle women over the border with Ukraine. When Géza heard about this, he went into the local bar where the gangster drank, and broke both of his arms. Upon making only the briefest of enquiries, the police learned that not one of the roomful of witnesses could remember having been present. For Géza there followed forty years of mending potholes, raising children and writing poems (he has many collections still in print). Now he lives in retirement on the slopes of Haláp, tending the vegetable garden, loudly despising the pre-ordained targets of the government-sponsored radio station, whittling a knife handle from a roe-deer horn, playing computer games, taking a shot of *palinka* before dinner for the sake of his digestion, and Skyping his grandchildren in Pécs. A twenty-first-century European.

Steven Lovatt's debut nonfiction title, *Birdsong in a Time of Silence*, is published in paperback in March by Particular Books.

BASS IN THE BLOOD

JODIE BOND RECALLS HOW SHE AND HER BROTHER
WEATHERED THE RUAL RAVE SCENE
CREATED BY HER FATHER, POST DIVORCE

FLASHING LIGHTS AND MUSIC WITH BASS THAT MADE THE EARTH SHAKE. A coven of five thousand, gathered for neon worship under a sky split open by helicopter search beams. This playground was not made for children. But this was the place I grew up; my childhood home.

It wasn't always this way. Before my parents separated, the old farmhouse was the definition of tranquility, nestled at the end of a valley, five miles from the nearest main road.

When I was eight years old, their divorce left this rural idyll in the hands of my father, who channelled his energies into transforming the hillside to become the beating heart of the nineties rave scene.

Dad is a kind man with a penchant for excess. He is a contradiction of personas: a public schoolboy; a hairdresser; a Lord of a micronation, an ex-con. He is gentle: quiet in the daytime, and more alive at night. He is a winning host: someone who makes friends easily and is generous to a fault. In the pub, locals would sidle up to him, knowing his propensity for offering the next round. He kept a stocked bar at home and would allow anyone to turn up unannounced and help themselves to whatever they liked. When guests commented that they liked things around the house, his natural reaction was to say, 'Do you want it? You should have it.' This, on occasion, had applied to my mum's belongings and my Christmas presents. His instinctive response to the divorce was to give. He wanted to host and to make people happy, feeling his way out of dejection by sparking the joy of a good party in others.

Dad's desire to surround himself with the masses, to be the king of the rave scene, was clearly triggered by the departure of my mum, but it was also a release. This had always been a part of his personality, a part he had kept dampened for the sake of a marriage. It had been bottled up for years, finding outlets in too many late nights at the bar, which left my mum stranded, alone with the children for too many nights for her to bear.

His absences made the tension between my parents mount, but I don't remember it that way. Early memories of a father trying to make amends through his children, beer on his breath as he would creep into my room, pressing a bag full of penny sweets into my sleeping hand. 'I love you, darling.' A kiss on my forehead. His charms always worked on me, though they failed on Mum, who soon left him for another man.

Dad's parties started small. Handfuls of friends, and friends of friends. All drawn here for the atavistic thrill of loosening inhibitions in a rugged landscape. The divorce had given Dad the perfect venue and he was keen to share it.

The internet was new and rich with niche communities, hungry for parties like this. As word spread, an infant web began to whisper about a valley in mid Wales that came alive at night. The crowds grew from dozens, to hundreds, to thousands. At their peak, they were the largest free raves in the UK.

The house was called Cyneiniog. As a child, it was my castle. A white stone building, thick walls and old slates, fronted by fields and backed by forest. I had the soles of a hobbit after years of running and playing on the jagged earth that made up the lane. It would take fifteen minutes to reach the nearest main road by car. Neighbours were sparse.

It was a place where you lived outside. The valley was refuge to a dwindling number of red squirrels. We watched foxes in the fields and listened to the shrieks of badgers by night. My childhood was spent catching frogs and hunting for bird nests. We walked, and rode horses, and on hot summer days we would splash through the deeper parts of the stream.

Land tamed by sheep and fences circled the garden, and beyond that, the sharp rise of the mountains. The house was nestled at the head of the valley, and the steep green slopes felt like walls that separated us from the real world.

Folklore tells us that the valley has always been home to a holy man. The mantle suited my father, who gave the role a New Age flare.

My brother and I would visit once a fortnight. We loved our time with Dad. He had more money than our mum and stepfather combined, and lavished us with a love that was both soft and financial. Trips to Woolworths were like being unleashed in Santa's grotto. I was given Barbies, Furbies, Tamagotchis, tickets to see the Spice Girls, the first iPod... all the things that so many of my friends, with their rural household incomes, could never afford. In the village Spar, we would fill our arms with as many sweets and chocolate bars as we could carry, our sustenance for the weekend. At Mum's, we were sustained by Suma wholefoods and had a twelve-inch television which could pick up three crackling stations. At Dad's, we gorged, hypnotised by satellite TV, our blood sugars rocketing.

He had a constant stream of friends who would stay for weeks or months. It was a commune of sorts, free of rules, where the adults all seemed to live for the weekend and often behaved like children. Late nights and early mornings, it would become my habit to crawl out of bed to complain to the grown-ups that their music was too loud or their laughter too much. Sometimes I found the scene very funny, too. Only eight years old, I didn't understand why one of his friends refused to come out of her bedroom one morning. She was wracked by shame. 'She was tripping,' explained Dad. 'She thought the dining room was a forest and pissed all over the carpet!' We both thought it was hilarious. Adults behaved very differently when they were around Dad.

Cyneiniog was transformed when the big raves started. Mum would worry. She wouldn't deny us our eager visit, but would argue with Dad about our safety. She wasn't wrong to do so. When I broke my arm, he didn't believe I was badly hurt. When my brother suffered third-degree burns, no one in the house was sober enough to take him to hospital.

The raves grew to international fame. This small farmhouse and its surrounding fields, which had mostly known sheep for company in the preceding centuries, were about to get a loud awakening.

The biggest rave of Dad's career was due to take place on a Saturday. My brother and I should have been returned home to Mum after a Friday night visit, but that had become an impossibility. The country lane was backed up with traffic. Too young to be walked all the way to the main road, we were trapped.

Mum fretted, but as children with little experience of the world and with a curiosity to match our inexperience, my brother and I were enthralled. We watched the vans unload six-foot speakers. Cargo netting was strewn in the outbuildings like Christmas decor, with swathes of it being hung in the outbuildings. Pegs were driven into sun-baked earth as bright big tops unfurled like surreal flowers in the fields. I sat on the wall outside the house and picked at the succulents that swelled to fill the spaces between stones. A man in patchwork trousers and a floral waistcoat ran towards the house and offered me a salute, 'Alright kiddo!' He grinned yellow teeth. The adults were ebullient and their elation was infectious. I watched swallows roll from the sky to their barn nests. They soared straight back out as the sound tests began. A shock of noise that made the battered barn roof vibrate. It made me jolt, then laugh. No wonder the adults were so excited.

Cars lined nose-to-tail along the five-mile lane that led to the house.

Drivers were forced to walk, leaving their vehicles stranded on a stony farm road. Their route took them through knots of forest, following a stream to a wide-bottomed valley which was overlooked by an abandoned slate mine with the air of an industrial castle. They would laugh, fizzing with excitement, a buzz of something else in their veins. Perturbed farmers were cut off, marooned in their havens, as the traffic mounted and the streams of people in wild dress journeyed along the valley. The motley caravan filled the air with the tin of battery-operated boom boxes and the green cloy of a thousand joints.

An abandoned waterwheel sat downstream of the house. My brother and I played together, splashing beside the remains of a rotting wooden wheel. We wanted to put ourselves out of the way. The steam rushed over the adult chatter, but didn't mask the bursts of music. From here, we could catch glimpses of people through the trees and, slowly, we watched our home transform. As the crowds streamed in, our wilderness became a strange and vibrant city. Kicking through the water, I imagined how the buzzards would see us all. People teeming in bright clothing, some moving disjointedly, others with the lightness of dance. A tapestry of people folding in and out of each other, the green hillsides eaten up by tents, vehicles and campfires.

I don't think we ate that evening. There wouldn't have been time. Besides, the kitchen had become headquarters for Dad's inner circle. Still, that excited chatter. Big grins on all faces. Tobacco and cannabis thickened the air.

The afternoon had delivered several of our friends into our care. All the children were bundled into my room while Dad set up a television for us. We were left with a selection of Disney VHSs and the strict order to 'be good and stay here'.

Children experience music differently at a certain volume. When the DJs started in earnest, the bass thudded through the earth. You could feel it in the walls of the house. We could feel it in our guts, in our bones.

It made me feel sick. Even now, Dad expresses mild alarm at the memory of the children being so physically affected by the bass. But there was no slowing this party down; it was in the hands of the masses. The music would be turned down for no one.

Our inaudible cartoons were occasionally disturbed by couples searching for a free bedroom. Sporadic visits from soft, pill-popping parents. Broad smiles and big black pupils, their faces painted like Celtic warriors. They told us how much they loved us and their words were bright with innocence.

The visits were infrequent enough and lacked enough discipline that we decided to put ourselves in charge. The adults were behaving hopelessly. Delighted orphans for a night, we decided to leave the confines of my room and explore the circus.

Five children, all under the age of ten. Like an illicit band of Blyton characters, we tumbled out of the house. In the twilight, bodies danced or sprawled on the grass. A cacophony of sound from warring DJs. The weekend's guests dressed like a tribe. Ripped clothes, tie-dye, face paint, wild hair. They moved by stumbling and dancing.

Coloured lights stretched out of the barns and stables, pooling as though it had fallen through stained glass on a different kind of church floor. Despite the body heat and the thrum of bass, we pushed ourselves into these spaces. Cigarettes and sweat. To my utter delight, I found I was glowing. My white T-shirt shone under UV. When I looked at my brother and our friends, their smiles were fluorescent. Murals had been painted on the walls. The largest of all was of a skeleton that appeared to burst through the stone walls of the barn, its eyes fierce under the strange lights. We picked up glow-sticks from a beer-pooled floor and waved them in the air, pretending to belong to this scene. Then the music changed tempo and everything flashed black-bright. The adults moved in a surreal staccato, like a stop-motion film. The strobes made our eyes hurt and we pushed our way back into the fresh air, relieved to be free.

Cars were everywhere they shouldn't be. I stopped to tell a group of drinkers to switch off their engine. 'You're polluting *my* grass.' They ignored the indignant child. Entrepreneurial ravers used their car boots as a lucrative business venture, selling pills and cans at inflated prices. Others pretended to be event managers, charging entry at the gates.

It was another world. The home that had always been so familiar to me had pulled on another guise, like the landscape had shifted into some otherworld. The veil had been torn down, revealing the true nature of the valley and the souls who had been drawn here.

Niall Griffiths brought his characters to this very party in his novel, *Sheepshagger*. His words bubble and flow, one of Wales' greatest wordsmiths conjuring personal experience of the party. He conjures a visceral description of the scene in his writing. His description of the scene holds a mirror to my memory.

> *In a natural bowl between an encircling rim of high hills is the main body of the rave with people swarming insectile and hive-like around tents and fires, strobes shredding the scene and the music rocking the thick-trunked old trees and the moon and the stars above it all and the ramshackle mansion up on the valley rise bursting blue then red from its windows, dancing silhouettes moving behind the glass, and from each of the throbbing marquees the beats of different musics merge and mix into one single mad euphony.*

We took in this scene, marvelling at the adults who had set up a playground that we couldn't understand. We witnessed people vomiting, fighting, and fucking in the fields. Unrestrained by societal conventions and with narcotics easier to come by than water, we saw tears, joy, fear. Ravers in the grips of euphoria; some rocking with paranoia, others collapsed, comatose. A few brief interactions made us feel celebrated. Wild children! We were special. Unique in this landscape. A woman stopped to tell us how she wished she had had a childhood like ours. Her words tangled and repeated. Her eyes hovered on the distance like they were gazing out of a window.

As the night wore on, we grew hungry. A vendor selling pick and mix from a van took pity on us and plied us each with a bag full of snacks.

Our parents weren't entirely neglectful. Throughout the night, they would feel the pull of responsibility and search for us. 'Are you alright?' they would ask. 'Isn't this wonderful? Shouldn't you get back to your room?' The dilation of their eyes had stripped all concern from them.

The night had spread its inkspill across the sky and we watched stars struggle through a new light pollution. In the space usually reserved for buzzards and kites, a police helicopter circled my home. I don't know what these parties cost the police, but they kept a close eye on Dad for years. When he was arrested for a relatively minor drink-driving offence some years later, we were all stunned to hear he had been given a prison sentence. The raves were entirely legal, but in the end, it seemed there was a price to pay for the trouble he had caused the authorities.

The music and flashing lights were too much to bear through the night. We were stretching our young bodies, forcing them to stay awake when they shouldn't be. As sleep dragged at our bones, we returned to my room. Screeching rewind on the VHS, we re-watched Disney. The television was at its highest volume and we raised our voices to hear each other as the house rocked with bass. We slept in snatches. Light sliced into the dark with the regular opening of the door. More couples peered in, looking for a bed. More people looking for a serviceable toilet. Our parents must have looked in on us, too.

On waking in the morning, we found sunrise had mellowed the scene. As Apollo took his first sip of coffee, so the DJs adjusted, softening to the new day. The tempo of the music had slowed. The police were gone. Though some still danced and drank and raved, more had fallen asleep. Many more sat wide-eyed, awake, but silent now, comedown stifling their energy.

The mountains scowled at fields littered with beer cans, plastic cups and fag ends. Between tunes, birds reclaimed the soundscape. As the sun reached its zenith, a slow exodus of people trickled from the valley. The lane to the house unblocked as cars retreated. We were free to return to the normality of our life with Mum.

Back to the world of tranquility, to homework, to nutritious meals, to early bedtimes. Our parents operated in parallel worlds. The environments they carved out for my brother and I have shaped us. Dad's upbringing taught us to be gregarious, fearless and generous, while Mum taught us kindness and openness, while keeping us grounded.

After the divorce, Mum gave me her old wedding ring. It bears the yin-yang symbol and I cannot think of a better emblem for their marriage. Through wild and tame, there was always joy, always love, and through their antithesis, they brought balance to their children. We were swept along on their pendulum of chaos and order, taking for ourselves the best of both worlds to shape the people we would become.

Jodie Bond is a writer, dancer and communications professional. She has worked for a circus and a gin distillery, and as a burlesque artist, as well as selling speciality sausages for a living, but her biggest passion has always been writing. *The Vagabond King*, her debut novel, was published by Parthian in 2019. jodiebond.co.uk

THANK YOU TO OUR
#SECURENEWWELSHREVIEW SUPPORTERS

Diamond Supporters:
Mary Chadwick
Professor Tony Curtis
Mary Oliver
Kaite O'Reilly

Platinum Supporters:
Tasha Alden
Ruhi Behi
E Clifford Cutler
Jasmine Donahaye
Elaine Ewart
Katie Gramich

Kurt Heinzelman
Gareth Lewis
Rhiannon Lewis
Susan Merriman
Jackie Morris
Dr Chris W Pitt
Jim Pratt
Tracey Rhys
Amy Strange
Clive Upton
Roger Williams
Carole Hailey

OVER EXPOSED

PHOTO-LANDSCAPE ESSAY BY
YVONNE REDDICK ON THE INSTAGRAM
CRASH SITE OF THE BLEAKLOW BOMBER

PHOTOS BY JONNY KINNEAR

A DISLOCATED WING, ITS RAGGED EDGE. AILERONS ROSE INTO THE AIR BEHIND two rusty engines. Clumps of sedge rooted on the flat aluminium panels of the fuselage. Some parts of the metal were bright as if new-polished, others were weathered to grey. The propeller shafts had begun to sink into the earth.

Nodules of molten metal lay scattered around the wing-fragments. When an RAF mountain rescue team found the wreckage, it was still burning.

On a misty day in March, my partner Jonny and I hiked to the crash site. We approached from Bleaklow's northern shoulder. We'd followed the Pennine Way to the heathery rise of Torside Castle. There, we'd seen a hare's path, winding through knee-high heath and whinberry. Our next waypoint was the Wain Stones. They don't look much like a hay-wain to me, though. Two of the gritstone boulders resemble faces in profile gazing at each other, with a third standing awkwardly beside them. The two craggy lovers are moving in for a kiss.

By the trig point at Higher Shelf Stones, Jonny and I paused, trying to get our bearings, at a pear-shaped boulder balanced on its end.

'Didn't the plane go down at the edge of the plateau?'

'Don't think we're there yet. The satellite image says we need to be further east.'

We peered at boot-prints, and the figures of other walkers wandering through the mist.

'Look!'

Jonny pointed to some twisted aluminium, grey against the black peat.

The US Air Force bomber *Over Exposed* was flying between air bases in November 1948 when low cloud obscured the way ahead. I know that low cloud in the Peaks – the dank mizzle that pulls a mosquito net over your eyes and seems to dampen your very soul. No one knows for sure

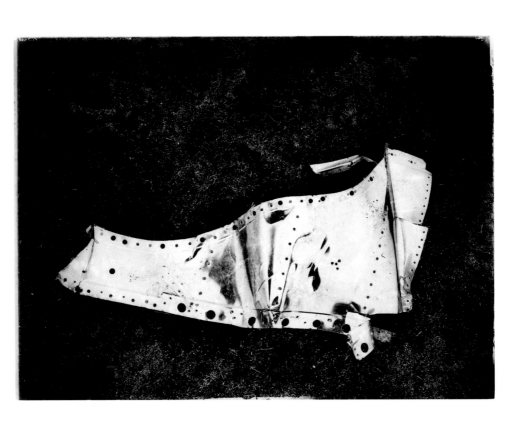

why the pilot, Captain Tanner, descended when he did. A glitch with the altimeter, a navigational slip, or maybe the cloud shrouding Higher Shelf Stones was enough. An RAF mountain rescue team were out on a training exercise that day, and they found the remains five hours after the plane hit the plateau. None of the thirteen men on board survived.

The moors make it easy for you to lose your way. When the mist descends, you can barely see your own boots, let alone the next tussock. New paths are eroded as old ones are abandoned. The high ground on Bleaklow and Kinder Scout is miles and miles of squelchy peat, criss-crossed by streams that change course and rough tracks made by sheep. Getting lost on Kinder Scout at nightfall is an unnerving experience. The time it happened to me, I wandered across featureless bog and heather, effing and blinding. No sodding phone signal, but my battery had packed up anyway. Nothing for it but to follow my compass. When the ridge of Win Hill and Lose Hill loomed into view, I almost laughed with relief. I've never been so happy to see the lights of the Rambler Inn.

Not everyone who loses their way is lucky enough to find it again. November 2020 saw six hikers being airlifted to safety after they set out to photograph what the media termed an 'Instagram crash site'. From Featherbed Moss to Cluther Rocks, many places in the Peak District are scattered with the wreckage of aircraft. What's left of the photographic reconnaissance plane *Over Exposed* is one of the Peak District's most photographed landmarks. It's inspired TikTok videos and Instagram hashtags. The crash site is visible in the satellite images that Jonny and I had used to navigate.

'Is this the way to the plane crash?' people asked on the Pennine Way. 'We're following ViewRanger, but the signal's run out,' said a man in Mountain Equipment outdoor gear, accompanied by his round-cheeked daughter and her smiling, dark-haired mother. People have worn short-cuts and desire paths from the Pennine Way to the wreckage; there were plenty of trails that my map knew nothing about.

Over Exposed got its name after it photographed an atomic weapons test on Bikini Atoll in 1946. In archival footage, sailors on board the ships surrounding the bomb test site crouch down and turn away, covering their eyes. Another Superfortress aircraft, *Dave's Dream*, drops the bomb. An atom-shattering flash. Aerial film shows the shockwave surging across the sea, then a halo of light. The fireball whooshes up; finally, a grey mushroom cloud ghosts into the upper air. All the ships the US Navy had stationed within half a mile were blasted to floating wreckage.

The peat surrounding the plane-wreck was pitted with footprints. Puddles and cigarette butts in indents in the metal. Walkers, most of them men, peered and pointed – 'That's a bit of fuselage.' One small boy bounced up and down on an aluminium panel near an engine. An empty Corona beer bottle lay abandoned on the ground.

Jonny snapped pictures of each of the four engines, then a view framed by a glassless window. The cold crept into my gloves. The Bleaklow bomber is a popular selfie site, but I was uneasy – were we trampling on a place that should be left in peace?

A plaque reads, 'IN MEMORY: Here lies the wreckage of CF B-29 Superfortress "Overexposed" of the 15th Photographic Reconnaissance Squadron USAF, which tragically crashed whilst descending through cloud…. It is doubtful the crew ever saw the ground.' In the shadow of a wing, a patch of bare earth, ringed with stones. Artificial poppies and wooden remembrance crosses sprouted out of the ground. The Stars and Stripes hung limply from upright wreckage. A photo with the caption, 'Remember Hoppy', a broad-jawed serviceman grinning breezily from the frame.

What draws people to peer at the plane's exposed anatomy? Maybe it's morbid and voyeuristic. Or perhaps it's about accepting that everything returns to earth, in the end.

IN MEMORY

HERE LIES THE WRECKAGE OF B-29 SUPERFORTRESS
"OVEREXPOSED" OF THE 16th PHOTOGRAPHIC RECONNAISSANCE
SQUADRON USAF WHICH TRAGICALLY CRASHED WHILST DESCENDING
THROUGH CLOUD ON 3rd NOVEMBER 1948 KILLING ALL 13
CREWMEMBERS. THE AIRCRAFT WAS ON A ROUTINE FLIGHT FROM
RAF SCAMPTON TO AMERICAN AFB BURTONWOOD.
IT IS DOUBTFUL THE CREW EVER SAW THE GROUND.
MEMORIAL LAID BY THE 6th NAVIGATION COURSE OF
RAF FINNINGLEY ON 12 NOVEMBER 1988

I remembered my father, who walked the Pennine Way when he was a young man. When I follow parts of the Pennine Way, as I often do in the Peak District, I have the uncanny feeling that I'm walking pace for pace alongside his jaunty, twenty-year-old ghost. In August 2015, he set off to hike alone in Scotland's Grey Corries, and never returned.

With each step of the path down from Higher Shelf Stones, the air felt warmer. A clough and a fence line led to the trig point on the next hill, where the landscape is riddled with disused quarries. The clean white bones of sheep. I set the compass to point a little west of north, to the Pennine Way. A curlew rose in flight, trailing its burbling call.

Many years after the plane crash, someone found a ring near the wreckage. It was Captain Tanner's wedding ring. The ring was returned to his daughter.

Yvonne Reddick holds an AHRC Leadership Fellowship for researching, publishing and writing poetry of the Anthropocene. Her publications include *Ted Hughes: Environmentalist and Ecopoet* and her poetry pamphlet, *Translating Mountains* (Seren, 2017), about the death of her beloved father and a close friend who both died while mountaineering. Her work appears in *The Guardian* (Review) and the *New Statesman*. yvonnereddick.org

Jonny Kinnear is a civil engineer by trade, with interests in sustainable drainage and flood risk management. Much of his spare time is spent outdoors, either hiking or cycling, and documenting these experiences through photography.

IN MEMORY

HERE LIES THE WRECKAGE OF B-29 SUPERFORTRESS
"OVEREXPOSED" OF THE 16th PHOTOGRAPHIC RECONNAISSANCE
SQUADRON USAF WHICH TRAGICALLY CRASHED WHILST DESCENDING
THROUGH CLOUD ON 3rd NOVEMBER 1948 KILLING ALL 13
CREWMEMBERS. THE AIRCRAFT WAS ON A ROUTINE FLIGHT FROM
RAF SCAMPTON TO AMERICAN AFB BURTONWOOD.
IT IS DOUBTFUL THE CREW EVER SAW THE GROUND.
MEMORIAL LAID BY 337 AIR NAVIGATION COURSE OF
RAF SHAWBURY ON 12 NOVEMBER 1988

VAGABONDAGE

RICHARD GWYN ON SOME RECENT TITLES
WHICH EVOKE THE MAGIC
OF THE TRAMPING LIFE

I HAD A FRIEND NAMED STUART, A VAGABOND BY VOCATION, WHO TOLD ME that when he was a child, a ragged, unkempt man once came to the door of the family home, and Stuart's mother gave him a few coins and an old coat that had belonged to her father. When the stranger had gone on his way, in answer to Stuart's persistent questioning, his mum told him that the man was a tramp. And what was a tramp? Someone, she explained (in simpler words) who has thrown all material aspiration to the winds, and walks the roads of the world without let or hindrance, a free spirit without a job or any of the responsibilities that society demands of adults. Stuart claimed that, from that day forth, his career plan took shape. Whether Stuart is still a tramp, I cannot say; one of the hazards (or dividends) of the tramping life is that by the very nature of their calling, individuals drift apart, lose touch, meet up again only by chance, or via the mysterious interventions of serendipity. You never know who you're going to bump into; you never know what's going to happen next.

In the Introduction to Ian Cutler's recent book, *The Lives and Extraordinary Adventures of Fifteen Tramp Writers from the Golden Age of Vagabondage* – the title itself a nod to the Golden Age of Long Book Titles – a useful distinction is made between three main varieties of vagrant:

> *A tramp is a man who doesn't work, who apparently doesn't want to work, who lives without working and who is constantly travelling. A hobo is a non-skilled, non-employed labourer*

without money, looking for work. A bum is a man who hangs
around a low-class saloon and begs or earns a few pennies a day
in order to obtain drink. He is usually inebriate.

This intriguing taxonomy, formulated by the one-time hobo and sociolo-gist Ben Reitman, is descriptive of the breeds of (male) vagrant found in the USA during and after the Great Depression but, as Cutler points out, the categorisation of tramps reaches back into the nineteenth century, the golden age of trampdom. Here is Charles Dickens, writing in 1860, warning of that most pernicious of impostors, the educated tramp:

The 'Educated' Tramp [is] the most vicious by far, of all idle
tramps... is more selfish and insolent than even the savage
tramp... this pitiless rascal blights the summer road as he
maunders on between luxuriant hedges; where to my thinking,
even the wild convolvulus and rose and sweetbriar are the worse
for his going by....

The term 'vagabond', meanwhile, in English at least, has archaic and Romantic connotations, and is now generally employed with a glimmer of irony. But the vagabond life has a lasting appeal and has spawned its own literary sub-genre, celebrated in a new series by the Feral House imprint, titled simply 'Tramp Lit', of which the two volumes under review form a part. The forerunners of the genre, writings by gentlemen of the road such as Morley Roberts (1857–1942), Trader Horn (1861–1931) and WH Davies (1871–1940), the Welsh author of *The Autobiography of a Super-Tramp*, are perhaps less well known now than they once were, though the claim to fame of Jack London (1876–1916) as a literary vagabond is well established: only last year 20th Century Fox released a megabucks production of *Call of the Wild*, starring Harrison Ford and a computer synthesised dog. (Less is said, in Cutler's account, about London's more unsavoury traits as a white 'Anglo-Saxon' supremacist: among the 'inferior' races denigrated by London, this icon of the freewheeling life includes the hapless Celt, who, he writes, 'wretchedly survives in a few isolated regions' (I guess that's us.)

Almost all of the tramps discussed by Cutler are men, with one notable exception: Kathleen Phelan (née Newton) was born in 1918 into a middle-class family with socialist leanings in County Durham; Ramsay MacDonald was a visitor to the family home and the young Kathleen was dandled on George Bernard Shaw's knee. From these auspicious beginnings, and after gaining a university degree, she spent a period teaching at the Rudolf Steiner school in Gloucester, but was soon smitten with wanderlust, and on one of her hitchhiking trips to the north of England, in 1944, she met a man waiting for a lift at the roadside near Garstang, Lancashire, but going the other way. According to her account, their exchange went as follows:

> He looked as though he hadn't a care in the world. High, wide and handsome. I had never seen anyone more colourful or alive-looking. He stood and looked at me a while, I stared back. Then in a deep, lilting, Irish voice, he said, 'And where might you be going.'
>
> Me – I said nothing, just kept looking.
>
> Then he spoke again. 'You didn't answer me. Where might you be going?'
>
> 'Nowhere,' I replied.
>
> 'I'm going there myself,' he said, 'Do you mind if I come along a bit of the way with you?'

Thus it was that Kathleen met Jim Phelan, rover, republican and ex-jail-bird: he had once been sentenced to death for his part in a bank robbery in which a man was killed, but the sentence was commuted to life imprisonment, following which he spent thirteen years in high-security prisons. Phelan was also, as chance would have it, a successful writer and journalist, and would take time off from his vagabondage to borrow a house from a seemingly endless list of well-wishers in order to knock off his next book. Kathleen hitched up with Jim and the two enjoyed this peripatetic lifestyle for over twenty years. These journeys make up the better part of her book, *There is Only One Road And It Goes Everywhere*. Whether or not due to Jim's tutelage, this first section, ending in Jim's death from lung cancer in 1966, is more fluently written than the note-book-type entries that cover the three years following Jim's death, and which recount Kathleen's solo travels, that took her through France and Spain, across North Africa to Egypt, Turkey, Iran, Afghanistan, Pakistan, India and Nepal. These entries are fragmentary, to say the least, and Kathleen never intended them for publication – this part of the book was compiled from notes found in her caravan following her death – with the result that what might have been the most interesting of vagabond autobiographies is ultimately a disappointment, as she reels off an abbreviated summary of her adventures. No amount of editing could make up for the fact that she lacks an eye for significant detail and seems unable to create a setting or succinctly develop a theme.

Far more interesting is the fact that she survived at all, given the attitude towards women travelling alone in many of the countries she visited. And despite her lack of writerly skills, Kathleen comes across as a beguiling character: the cover blurb refers to her as a 'real life Amélie' and there is something of the ingénue about her: an appealing, strong-willed but somewhat feckless woman to whom stuff happens. Except in Kathleen's case, the events often totter on the edge of the credible. An example would be her crossing of the Himalayas on foot, when the narrative takes on a haphazard, surreal tone: after climbing the pass from Luhri to Ani in freezing conditions (and without suitable clothing) she joins a group of Tibetan refugees and their forty ponies, before descending to the Kuala valley where a festival is in progress: 'The whole valley was a kaleidoscope of colour. Every village sent its idol, carried by the local people who did a kind of dervish dance with daggers drawn. What a scene!' The account is peppered by such exclamations of wonderment, as we are told, rather than shown, the unfolding events with interjections of 'Incredible!' 'Hilarious!' 'Amazing!' After a while, remarkable as her experiences are, sharing in Kathleen's expressions of astonishment becomes a tad wearisome, as she cannot skilfully elicit the scenes she summarises. Her pages are filled with this kind of telling, as when she spends several days crossing the desert on a water train, perched on one of the container trucks before arriving at a remote settlement:

> *I climbed down the ladder and made my way across to the building. A group of people rushed out. If I had been a Martian I could not have been a greater sensation. A very official-looking person came up to me. He wore a peaked cap and lots of gold braid.*
>
> *'I have worked here for thirty years,' he said, 'and I have never seen anything like this happen before. A woman!'*

For the last three decades of her life, Kathleen moved from one caravan site to the next, up and down the Britain and Ireland. She made many friends and was much loved, dying at the age of ninety-six – seventy years after that meeting with Jim Phelan on the road outside Garstang. Liam Phelan (Jim's grandson from an earlier marriage) eloquently sums up Kathleen's legacy in his Foreword: 'She was a pioneering woman, living life on the road facing the prospect of sexual assault and death. She was fiercely independent and held her own among rough and sexist men with ease. But she never made a big deal out of it. She shrugged off the danger.'

* * *

Ian Cutler's study of Jim Christy, subtitled A Vagabond Life, is another curio, put together from interviews with the author and interspersed with lengthy extracts from Christy's many books. One might question the motives for writing a biography of a still living writer of undeniable charisma but – on the basis of the extracts included here – unexceptional talents, especially since most of Christy's writings are themselves autobiographical. The result, more than anything else, is an anecdotal confection, which often repeats itself, if not in actual content, at least in the manner of its telling. Cutler employs a narrative style of stops and starts, interrupted repeatedly by comments such as 'but to return to 1962', 'but back to our own hero in 1967' or 'but more of boxing and Stallone later'; there are dozens of these asides that build up into a recurrent irritation, as Cutler attempts to produce a storyline that is far from seamless, and which remains consistent only in his unquestioning and uncritical, even adulatory, attitude towards his subject. We learn from Christy himself that, at the age of eight, he was deemed to be 'reading at the level of a second-year university student', which adds to the growing awareness that, for all Christy's gifts, modesty does not rank among them. He comes across as a shrewd, observant and restless individual, and occasionally a thought-provoking writer (but a pretty lousy poet) whose self-belief, however, outweighs his literary achievement.

As a teenage runaway, Jim Christy took to the road with the exiled Russian Count Navrotolov or Navratilini – 'Christy can only accurately recall the "Nav" part of the name' – better known by his sobriquet Count Garbage, because of his proclivity for poking around in rubbish; he played pool with the then Vice President Lyndon B Johnson, took part in the Selma race riots, worked on the numbers racket for a Sicilian mafia boss, dodged the draft, 'had a fling' with Janis Joplin and was embraced ostentatiously by Muhammad Ali. In spite of his disdain for hippies, he hung out in Haight-Ashbury during the summer of love in 1968, of which he wrote: 'I was bored with the entire scene. It just seemed like a massive convention of conventional suburban kids taking some time out from their schooling and their careers to gather their future nostalgia.' While lacking Joan Didion's incisiveness (the sharpest of observers in deconstructing the hippy myth in her essay 'Slouching Towards Bethlehem'), Christy was all too aware that many of the passive participants in the sexual revolution and the much-vaunted 'free love' of the times – mainly young women – were in fact victims, 'prey for the opportunists, the rapists, the crooked drug dealers, the guru hustlers, crooks of all sorts.' Christy's anecdotes are conveyed in a wry, subversive voice that, at its best, effectively captures the spirit of the times. Almost inevitably, after reading *On The Road,* he falls under the spell of Jack Kerouac. The Beats, and Kerouac especially, provided a breath of fresh air for this unruly youth stifled by the rules and constraints of bourgeois suburbia, and headed for a life of unbridled adventure outside the law (and occasionally enjoying the hospitality of its penal institutions). Nevertheless, in Cutler's account, there is something monotonous about the stream of vagabond anecdotes that emerge, populated by men with names like Jim and Jack, heading for the open road, getting into fights, tramping around in a manly (and often misogynist) bid for freedom. Freedom from what, exactly? Cutler claims that once we were all tramps, that the human race is essentially nomadic: but nomads, that is, nomadic peoples, have a world vision that is not based on a desire to escape from dull, conformist society; rather, nomadism is a cultural norm for the people who live in those societies; perhaps for them the rebel would be the one who decided to stay put.

Anyone who spends a long time living on the road accumulates fantastical, absurd and sometimes terrifying adventures, to the extent that a certain expectation of the extraordinary becomes the default. To those whose lives are circumscribed by conventional societal norms, any day in the life of the homeless tramp would be exceptional, but – if you're going to tell stories about this sort of life – they will only be as interesting as the manner in which they are told; no matter how many metaphorical exclamation marks the author puts in place, and no matter how many declarations of 'Incredible!' 'Hilarious!' 'Amazing!' a writer offers, nothing can substitute for well-crafted, nuanced sentences and layered characters. Especially – in a biography – the latter.

I have done my fair share of tramping, and in contrast to the rhapsodic belief voiced in Christy's story, and in Tramp Lit generally, that the vagabond life is never dull, I found it frequently to be so. As I've suggested elsewhere, the single most resounding memory of my years spent as a vagabond are of immense tedium, waiting around for something to happen. Then there are the nights in the slammer, the verbal abuse and occasional violence, the taunts and ridicule of certain tradespeople and 'members of the public' – of whom you are effectively no longer one, as you are often reminded.

But that is not the whole story, and – on the plus side – there were the occasional extraordinary acts of kindness and of courage, as well as the immensely seductive pull of the open road, the unique sensation that no one on earth knows what you are doing at a given time, nor where you are, nor where you are headed, and in that knowledge lies a peculiar sense of serenity and release. But release from what? What is it that diehard vagabonds wish to escape, if not, at least in part, themselves? Cutler makes a case for the vagabond philosophy as an expression of classical Cynicism, as practised by Diogenes (who lived in a barrel, or a tub, and famously asked Alexander the Great to step out of the light) with a dollop of Nietzsche thrown in, but I am unconvinced that many of the clochards I encountered in the dosshouses of France would conform to this type.

The beauty of the tramping life lies precisely in that sense of faith in serendipity, of accepting what will happen – and in the delight of starting each day with no idea of what will befall you; no idea of where you will spend the next night; no idea of who you might meet or what you might encounter. That, in essence, is the magic of vagabondage, and this, rather than any claims to literary excellence, is the quality these two books abundantly evoke.

Richard Gwyn is the author of *The Vagabond's Breakfast*, winner of the 2012 Wales Book of the Year for Nonfiction and published by Alcemi. His most recent novel is *The Blue Tent* (Parthian, 2019).

Titles Discussed
There is Only One Road and it Goes Everywhere by Kathleen Phelan (Feral House, 2020)
Jim Christy: A Vagabond Life by Ian Cutler (Feral House, 2019)

RETURN TO WATER

MEMOIR EXTRACT ON SWIMMING AND BODY
CONFIDENCE BY **KATHRYN TANN**

II

THE SKY IS BRIGHT THIS MORNING, AND, AS I SWAN THROUGH THE CENTRE of the pool, beams of light quiver in the cloudy blue in all directions. Another swimmer arrives. I break into my front crawl, find my rhythm, and let my thoughts roll on with the soft momentum of my strokes. One, two, three, breathe. One, two, three, breathe.

In my family, I'm the runt of the litter, the youngest of four; and they all insist that I was a water baby. My mum remembers early bath-times: I would get very excited, frantically waving arms and legs, happily splashing water out of the plastic baby-bath. I can recall some of this excitement a few years later in the big tub. I would refuse to get out; instead relentlessly sliding up and down the ceramic on my bum, until all the water had drained away and I could slide no more.

Both my mum and dad remember clearly the arguments over who was to take us to the local pool. Neither of them looked forward to the weekly Sunday outings. 'It was stressful', she said, 'keeping an eye on you all. Your brother almost drowned on multiple occasions, and I'm sure there were rules about how many children you could supervise alone. We were always breaking that.'

What I remember are the orange armbands that pinched your skin going on, the nappy-smell in the changing rooms, the colossal slide that shot you out into the pool at what felt like a million miles an hour.

Slipping through the water now, it's strange to think that this move-ment needed learning. It's come to be so natural: my body adjusts to the gravitational change like a bird taking thoughtlessly to air.

My dad is often there in my most memorable swimming moments – he was the person I followed into most adventures. I remember when he lowered me down into a container tank at work and let me doggy-paddle in the dark. My dad's company – a chemical manufacturer in Barry Docks – had just had a new storage tank delivered to the warehouse. It was a huge black metal block of a thing, as big as a house to my young eyes. Regulations meant that the tank had to be leak-tested, which involved filling it up with water and letting it sit for fourteen days. He saw this as an opportunity: why waste all that clean water? So he asked if any of us wanted to go for a swim.

Thinking it sounded like a brilliant idea, I was the only volunteer. I remember my mum and sister standing on the top of the tank with Dad as he lowered me down through the small opening and into the pitch black water – which, of course, was very cold. I loved it. I giggled away, treading water in my armbands, a little scared of the void around me but never willing to admit it.

Sometimes, when I visit Dad's work, I walk past that tank, sitting there now under a layer of dust, holding huge quantities of aluminium chlorohydrate. I'm taken, fleetingly, back to that bizarre evening, and it feels as though I could have dreamt the whole thing up.

By the time I was nine, I had decided that *natural* water was a thor-oughly magical place to be. We went on a trip that year, to Canada, and through my lake-tinted glasses, the fortnight spent travelling the Rockies was really just a swimming tour. The memory I always return to from then comes from one of the last days: we had parked up by a lake for lunch, and I had managed to wangle permission to go off and find the jetty. Once there I left my sandals by a well-worn log and ran. My feet barely skimmed the wooden planks and when I reached the end I didn't stop, I didn't hesitate; I just jumped. I could feel hundreds of tiny bubbles fizzing about me, rolling up my skin and tickling my cheeks. This immediate, carbonated aftermath of jumping in was, and still is, one of my absolute favourite sensations.

I opened my eyes in the fresh green water and found myself surrounded by flashing fish. I had jumped straight into a shoal of them, and as they flitted about I felt one brush my ankle, my arm, escape my hair. I stayed suspended for a moment, and then reluctantly resurfaced. This is a memory I have painstakingly preserved, because it was perfect. Most thrilling was the fact that it belonged entirely to me and no one else. It was the first in a collection of moments in which I have been completely and blissfully present, in my body, cushioned from everything but myself, my happiness, and my glorious surroundings.

Any water would do, of course. Though we lived by the sea (the silty Severn Estuary, often out of reach beyond half a mile of mud), good natural swimming holes weren't too common. When I was seven, however, we moved to a house which could more easily fit all of us under its roof. And quite bizarrely, at the bottom of its garden, this house had a swimming pool. A survival of the fifties or sixties, lino-lined and rectangular, but very much still usable. On finding this out, the idea of having to leave my beloved home (the one I had been born in) became much less of an injustice.

From then on, I would spend my summer holidays in a constant state of either dripping-wet or drying-off. Friends would visit every day; I'd zoom lengths with my second-hand flippers; I'd dive for 'treasures' (a precious array of heavy plastic objects). We had an old long dressing-up box which my siblings and I turned on its end and used as a diving platform... a health-and-safety disaster, considering the pool was just over a metre deep. One year, we bought an inflatable slide for the poolside, but quickly discovered it was much more fun when used upside down, in the water, as a giant floating seesaw we could all pile onto at once. The plastic was split before the summer's end.

I was eleven when I first looked at a photo snapped during one of these mad pool-parties, and felt unhappy about how I looked. This was before I had started wearing makeup, before I even really thought about my appearance from an outward perspective. But I clearly remember seeing my red face, goggled eyes, crooked teeth, and wet rat-tailed hair, and I remember the image resurfacing in my mind when I next swam with my friends. It was then that I lost it: my sense of abandon slipped away. Water was becoming more complicated.

III

I concentrate for a while on my breathing, on the shape of my hands as they enter the water, the frequency of my kicks and the strand of hair which I can never prevent from plastering my face each time I turn to take in air. Swimming lengths is an easy way to be alone with your own mind. There's respite in the simple pattern of my movements, in the drag and ripple of my body as I swim. One, two, three, breathe. One, two, three, breathe.

I inherited the family tendency for acne at around the age of twelve. With it came a host of problems and anxieties, which across the years were mixed in with a cocktail of other adolescent battles, inextricable from one another and, ultimately, quite impactful on my way of life. I had a tricky and fragile relationship with my outward appearance, and it was the kind of unhealthy relationship that stopped me from being myself, from doing certain things, and from having certain conversations.

This is a story shared, I know, by many. And in every version, there's a private goal-post: the thing you always spend your wishes on. What I'm doing now – swimming lengths in a standard chlorinated swimming pool, flanked by passing strangers – was mine.

When I was thirteen, I started wearing makeup every day – despite not knowing what to buy or how best to put it on. I had by that point fully acquired my 'problem skin', and the result was a growing sense of disconnection with my own appearance.

I would say that makeup was my mask, but it wasn't: the version underneath – the red and sore and angry version that met the mirror before bed – that wasn't me. I couldn't be myself (I didn't have the guts) without the armour of my curated appearance, the careful ritual of my morning routine. Makeup gave me the freedom to face the world with confidence, and each year that my skin grew worse, it trapped me tighter into my dependence on those products.

And so it came to be that I couldn't submerge myself in water anymore. Of course I couldn't. It would jeopardise the careful control I thought I needed: it would wash away all that held me up.

It was in my fourteenth year that I grew out of starring in the local pantomime; but I have a much-avoided memory of that final show which marks a point of no return. I had a friend that year – a little girl in the cast who had taken a shine to me and liked to follow me around. Her name was Florence and she was six years old. One evening, as I played with her in the village hall, I noticed her gaze become fixed on my mouth and jaw. This was a particular problem area for me. What Florence did next was more awful than anything I had faced before: she reached her hand up as I was talking, as if to touch my inflamed skin. Instinctively I caught her arm and gave it back to her, trying to continue on as if all was normal. But then, eyes still fixed, she said, 'What's that?'

'What's what?' I replied, pretending to be oblivious.

'What's that on your face?' she said.

I could have calmly explained to this little girl that acne is something that lots of people experience, that it's quite normal, if slightly frustrating. But I was mortified. Florence had done what I feared most in the world: she had noticed. She had made me naked to attention, ruined the whole façade. I caught another outstretched hand and told her not to point. 'You shouldn't say that to people,' I said. 'It's rude.' For the rest of the rehearsal, I let my hair fall onto my face, and tucked my chin into my favourite sparkly scarf. I felt, as I would feel for many more years, a desperate need to hide my skin. Until that point, I had often told myself that other people might not see it, that my cheerful self and buoyant voice would camouflage my insecurities. Florence had meant no harm of course – she had only said what she was thinking. But this was the problem: it meant that other people thought the same, they just didn't dare to say it.

As I grew older, I learnt how best to hide. I was good at it. No one would have said I was a shy girl. My mum understood how important makeup was to me, and for that I will always be so grateful. She helped me buy the right products, researched with me, supported me when I couldn't pay for the skin-sensitive ranges – and took me to the GP when I had appointments for my acne. Gradually, I honed my skills and was able to make it all look 'natural' for school.

The years I spent hiding, I also spent pretending there was nothing to hide. Even my language was part of the effort. I couldn't bring myself to utter certain words, or make any kind of reference to my skin. Spots, acne, pimples, zits: even typing them here makes my body tense and flinch. Each word had the power to break the spell, to make me suddenly bare to other people's searching eyes. I never talked about it to my friends. I never took my makeup off. I never drew attention to this fact. I lived in complete outward denial of the thing that, secretly, ruled my life.

It was easier to forget how much I loved to swim: much easier to forget than live in constant conflict with it. I stopped visiting the local pool – that was far too stressful. I could still go to the sea with friends, but I had to turn myself into the person who only waded in so far, while others splashed and messed about. The few times I was invited for a Friday night at the big new pool with curly slides and disco lights, I made my excuses. To be wet was to be anxious – it reminded me of the fragility of my performance. I didn't belong to my own bare skin. Swimming no longer gave me power, it threatened it.

* * *

One September afternoon, a week or so before second year at university began, Dad and I went for a cycle to the sea. It was a sunny day in Pembrokeshire, and we were heading for our favourite bay, just along the coast from the stack rocks at St Govan's. By the time we hit the grassy path leading down the hidden valley, we were hot and tired and unstoppable. This wedge of coast has water as clear and turquoise as the Mediterranean – though somewhat colder. Our secret little beach – blasted into existence in World War II, and now tucked safely beyond a WARNING: EXPLOSIVES military sign – is a swimmer's small paradise.

We left our clothes on the rocks, socks tucked safely into trainers, and met the Atlantic at a sprint. It soon slowed me into an eager wade, and when my thighs twitched in sharp reaction, I threw my shoulders in.

Dad swam further out to the mouth of the bay. I let myself drift and tread until my toes could no longer scrape the sand. I leant back, felt my hair spread, the back of my head cradled by the cold. I let my feet float to the sunny surface, my ears go under, and all was quiet. I could hear the muffled whooshing of my circling hands. My eyes fixed on the sky. I stopped paddling with my feet and let my body be held by the salt water. The rocky walls of our secret bay climbed into my peripheries each time the swell fell away.

My hands started making swirls in the water again as I worked to keep my face above the surface. I thought of my friends earlier that summer, diving into the waves in Cornwall while I waded in and prayed at least some of my waterproof foundation would survive. They spent the whole week showing their faces to the sun, gathering salt and freckles on their skin. 'Why would I wear makeup? I'm on holiday! I'm having a break from all that.' They didn't know how alien such a thought was to me. They didn't know how the words, thrown into the room like laughter, made me ache. I've never been more violently jealous than I was in that minute.

I could see Dad diving under, resurfacing, shaking the droplets from his lashes and swimming without a care. I closed my eyes and pushed the sea above my face. Surrounded by it, completely, for the first time in years, I swam without thinking. I let myself be present in that simple, water-induced way. I swam without my old, relentless, illogical fears, and I didn't collect them again until we came laughing back to the shallows.

Kathryn Tann, from the Vale of Glamorgan, worked until recently for Parthian Books, taking up a new role in autumn with New Writing North. She has an MA in Creative Writing from the University of Manchester and a BA in English Literature from Durham University. She writes short fiction and creative non-fiction, and recently completed her first novel, *When We Arrive*. Her work has appeared in the Penfro winner's anthology, *Heartland* (2019), MANY: *The Manchester Anthology* (2020), *Cheval 13* (2020), *Lucent Dreaming* and online publications including *Porridge* magazine and *Santes Dwynwen*, as well as a recent audio essay for *Litro* magazine. Kathryn founded the Podcast for New Writing in Manchester, and received a Distinguished Achievement Award while studying as a postgraduate there. She was named a Printing Charity 'Rising Star' and Bookseller 'Rising Star' in 2021 and her work in publishing includes the development of the first Parthian podcast and audiobook list, and a focus on diverse voices. 'Return to Water' is an abridged extract from a longer memoir, which was her highly commended entry in the New Welsh Writing Awards 2021 Rheidol Prize for Prose with a Welsh Theme or Setting. She was also joint winner, with Penny Lewis in the 18-25 year-old category of this prize.

THE LOVESPOONS

EXTRACT BY **PENNY LEWIS**

THE BLACK-PAINTED WROUGHT-IRON KISSING GATE SQUEAKED WEAKLY LIKE A trapped mouse as Dawn pushed it to and then back. She was visiting her old friends. The terrier was being difficult, refusing to follow her heels.

'Come on,' Dawn said, tugging the taut lead around the gate.

The chapel was a whitewashed stone presence, bright in the mid-morning sun. It stood before the graves. Above its two doors was a circular window. The dusky pane of glass looked down at Dawn. Along either side of the block-shaped building were three long doleful windows.

Twenty years ago, on her first Sunday in Coed Newydd, Dawn had stepped inside this chapel. Then, the pews had been full. Two months ago, on the last funeral, there had only been a handful of folk. Now the doors were locked.

Dawn was sure that, at one time, a year would have seen many services, dotted with christenings and weddings. The magnificence of the organ; the wholesome hymns. She had been told that everyone in the village had their place in the chapel; their family pew or balcony. She imagined her friends, all in their youth, dressed in their Sunday best, and gathering. The women in shin-length dresses and the men in woollen suits. In the winter, bundled in coats, scarfs and hats, they would be sheltered within the sturdy walls from the wind. And in the summer, they would welcome the coolness of those walls.

Those bygone days were past when she had arrived in Coed Newydd, but Sunday chapel had still been well attended. Dawn wasn't a religious woman, but she had fair valued the weekly ritual of chapel. She had fair loved offering tea and homemade cake for her friends, afterwards.

The graveyard was in a terrible state, out of Dawn's control. Rags of moss scattered the path and misshapen hands of lichen grappled the low drystone walls. Ivy was beginning to climb some of the tombstones.

Something caught on her skirt. It was a bramble, with thorns the size of fingernails. Dozens of the inch-thick things were creeping in from the riverside.

Other than unruly holiday-maker children, no one but Dawn ever came here now. No one swept back the pebbles, no one mowed the grass, no one had cleared away the flowers. The flowers were nothing but brown leeches clinging down the sides of their square pots.

A Welsh word occurred to her. Sometimes they did, appearing in her head unpreceded by English translation. Chwyrligwgan. Chw-url-ee-goo-gan, Morfudd would pronounce. it Now, what did it mean? Something, she thought, to do with life? The word had appeared out of nowhere, as if she had subconsciously seen it on a tombstone. Chwyrligwgan, chwyrligwgan. She would have remembered what it meant if she was still surrounded by her friends, encouraging her, prompting her with new words. But now she no longer had anyone to speak the language with. Only herself.

The language had been entirely new to her when she had arrived in the village. She had been plunged into a Shakespearian play, with everyone around her speaking this poetry so perfectly. The words had sounded almost exotic to Dawn, but also comforting. Welsh had a cadence like no other language.

Chwyrligwgan: merry-go-round. The village was once a carousel, with music and laughter and light. Cars and motorbikes had replaced the artistic gallopers, and now the dead place was a modern speedway.

Learning the language had been so rewarding, like picking fruit. Challenging, but it had made her younger. It had woken her up. And the names – she had been so tongue-tied over their names. Trying to remember them all, and the syllables, in the correct sequence, had been like keeping a handful of boiled sweets in her mouth and trying to speak. There had been so many folk to get to know. Twenty years hadn't been nearly enough.

To help learn their names, she would write them out over and over again, carrying them all in her mind like an apronful of apples. Olwen, she remembered, because she had been so much like an owl, always perched reading in the third-storey window of her house. Bronwen, she had brown hair. Nerys, because she was nice. Glyn, like a 'glen', a valley. Now, as she stood before all the headstones, all these names were written out, level with her knees.

Step at a time, she passed Ifanwy Jones, Nerys Havard, Dafydd Hughes, Rhoswen Ellis, Morfudd Davies. Poor Morfudd, who had caught such a bad cold. So soon after, Sioned had gone, and with her, Olwen. Death had rolled like a lead ball through the village. Door after door after door. Her friends' names had dropped from house to grave like falling apples. Thud, thud, thud, and a final THUD – when the chapel doors had shut tight after the last funeral. Dawn closed her eyes and took a painful breath of the damp air. Loneliness was an internal claustrophobia, like heartburn.

The rows of tombstones ended and the raggedy grass began. Here was where the pets had always been buried. It didn't follow regulations to bury animals so close to the graves of people, but this was Coed Newydd, and the villagers were strong willed here. They had always argued that the patch of land was theirs and not the chapel's. No one would dispute the matter now.

The terrier quaked on the path, gazing blankly at the matted grass before it. It was time to go. Dawn turned back, the leash tautening in her grip before the terrier followed, past the chapel and back through the gate.

The river was gentle today. It was half the size it had been before, and the water was clearer. There was a crack. Dawn peered over the railing at what seemed to be a binbag shifting in the breeze. More litter.

But the binbag got up, and Barry's dull bald head and hunched shoulders appeared. Dawn almost said hello, but restrained herself, and was glad of it a moment later when Barry somewhat angrily snapped a branch. He threw it, and swore horribly.

Dawn shifted back from the railing, brushing her mouth nervously with the back of her hand. Her slip-on shoes squeaked against each other, the terrier whined loudly. She quickly turned around to pretend to be looking upstream.

With threatening glance at the terrier, that gazed up at her dumbly, Dawn peered over the downstream edge. Barry hadn't heard her.

Barry was now bent down, rummaging in the twigs and muck left by the river's last splurge. Stretched over his puffy white hands were black fingerless gloves. They looked far too small for him, as if he had never given up wearing them since he was a child. Dawn considered, he could fair do with a proper pair of gloves.

He wrestled a branch out, turned it in his hand, snapped it and drew his arm back. Dawn stepped back. The two broken pieces of the branch split apart in mid-air and landed far downstream. One jumped pathetically out of the water, before they were both carried away.

Barry lurched at the banking, grabbed a fistful of overgrown grass and attempted to haul himself up. Dawn hesitated, stepping back and then forward as she watched him struggle. The terrier whimpered, and she looked sharply at it.

Then Barry got hold of the trunk of a tree, and – with a grunt – he heaved himself to get a heel wedged over one of the bulging roots. The tree looked dead, and Dawn stepped forward, her mouth involuntarily opening.

But Barry was already swiftly clambering on his hands and knees over the rise of the banking and Dawn was caught on the bridge. Heart pounding, she hurried away. Halfway up the hill, she glanced back at the footbridge. Barry was there, wiping his hands on his trousers and looking at her. Dawn fixed her eyes on the road. The terrier crossed in front of her and she stumbled to avoid treading on its paws.

Around the bend at the top of the hill, she hurried the rest of the way home, cursing the terrier now trotting at her heels. She tugged its lead irritably.

* * *

Dawn put the kettle on the stove, and got her cup and saucer ready. It was her usual, taken from her Bluebell Woods tea-set. For months, this cup and saucer had been the only one that had been used. Dawn supposed that she ought to rotate them. Get another one out. The weeks went by so quickly.

Sat at the table with her brewing pot of tea, Dawn looked at her lovespoons. How still they were, so gentle.

She wondered what kind of place Barry's house, Y Slant, was inside. It was a similar build to the miners' houses, but perhaps bigger. She couldn't imagine it being anything different to those houses. Good fireplaces. Tiled floors. Unpainted wooden staircases.

Dawn considered, if there were no curtains, then table covers, tea towels and other homely touches were unlikely. If there were no lightshades, perhaps there wasn't much there for furniture. She supposed it was the last of the grander houses in the village that hadn't been ruined by holiday home owners.

The tap was incessantly ticking. Rapidly and anxiously. It never stopped, no matter how she tightened it. Dawn reached forward for the teapot.

It suddenly went quite dark. What odd weather, she thought, thinking it a passing rain cloud. But it wasn't a rain cloud at all – it was Barry, in his big coat, almost filling her back window. Her hand holding the teapot jolted, spilling a copper pool onto the saucer.

How odd Barry looked today! Half-moon crown of long hair, expressionless, wide eyed; eyes which were darker-rimmed than before. Dawn carried the teapot all the way to the back door, where she realised she was still clutching it and spun around to put it down.

She burst open the door.

'Barry!' she said, seeing him holding out yet another lovespoon. 'I gave that back to you!'

'It's only small, it's only small, you'll have room for it somewhere.'

Dawn searched his face, but nothing could be read in his absent smile, permanently knotted brow, and bright blue bulging eyes. The gaze of those eyes drifted and darted about above Dawn's head like bees, and shifted sideways at her glance.

Dawn purposefully ignored the lovespoon he held out. Excitedly, she asked, 'Did you like the butterfly buns?'

Barry raised his eyebrows. It was the first conventional sign of emotion Dawn had seen in him.

She panicked. 'I hadn't iced them too much, had I? I never know how much icing folk like…?'

Barry pushed his massive paw, holding the lovespoon, towards Dawn's hand at her side. The wood brushing her knuckle, she swiftly whipped her hand behind her back.

Barry said, 'I didn't know you'd made them.'

'Made them? Of course I made them!'

Barry said nothing.

'Who else?'

The lovespoon was now in his other paw. Dawn's sweating hands met behind her back, locking fingers.

He didn't respond. Dawn sighed, 'Barry, did your father make that lovespoon?'

Barry looked down at his old leather boots, then back up at Dawn with a sort of wry smile. 'Does it matter?' he asked.

Dawn, completely losing his meaning, shook her head. Was that cheekiness in his faint smile? Too late. It was gone. 'Barry... perhaps I ought to be plain with you,' she began. 'I'm, I'm too old for this –'

Barry's face wrinkled like a scrunched ball of paper. The bags beneath his eyes were bluish-black. 'Do you want it or not?' he said, returning to the first attempt of offering it somewhat lackadaisically. To hold a work of art so carelessly!

Dawn rubbed her forehead, feeling how thin her hair was. Barry's face was blank. She found she could no longer look at his face. The rounded mound of his upper back, that he couldn't seem to straighten, gave Dawn the impression he was already bored.

'Don't you want it yourself?' she asked.

Barry said nothing. Dawn tried, 'What will you do with it if I don't take it?'

Blandly, he said, 'I want you to have it.'

Dawn held her breath, then let it out. 'But Barry, it's too kind of you, too kind....'

Barry slipped the lovespoon between her fingers, stopping her from unconsciously wringing them.

'Barry!' she called to the back of his balding head and sloping shoulders. She was direct about it. 'Why are you letting go of things? You're not selling up, are you?'

'I want you to have it!' he yelled, and he batted away her words with a strong back-swing of his arm.

Dawn took a step after him, but realised she was wearing her house slippers, and had no choice but to retreat inside.

In a tumult of dismay, confusion and embarrassment, Dawn hung the lovespoon in the place she had imagined it would go so nicely, above the other three. The poor unwanted thing was like an underfed robin taken in from the cold as it warmed in her kitchen.

Had Barry really wanted to get rid of these four lovespoons? A lifetime's work? His father's work?

Perhaps Barry was bored. Perhaps he enjoyed giving gifts. That was all. Perhaps he had nothing else to give, and was giving away things that were precious to himself. Dawn could never be so generous herself. She would never give away her Bluebell Woods tea-set. How selfish she was!

And, to her agony, she remembered how she had said those silly words 'I'm too old for this!' Her head throbbed in embarrassment.

Barry had pulled his face in that way. But it still meant nothing. Was it embarrassment? Disgust? He had only said, 'I want you to have it.'

What did that mean?

Their conversation clattered about in her head.

Penny Lewis was born and grew up in Aber-arth, Ceredigion. During her A levels, she was awarded a scholarship to study on a two-week writing course at Harvard University. She has also been an assistant at the unmatched Ystwyth Books, Aberystwyth. When school ended abruptly with lockdown in March 2020, she began writing seriously, entering the New Welsh Writing Awards: Rheidol Prize for Prose with a Welsh Theme or Setting the following year with a submission (extracted here) that was highly commended.

NEEDLEWORK

NOVEL PREVIEW FROM *FANNIE*
BY **REBECCA F JOHN**

THE SUPERVISOR ARRIVES AT THE FACTORY TO FIND FANNIE UNFOLDING HER second garment. She watches from the doorway for a moment as Fannie, head bent as elegantly as a poised carriage horse, smooths the indigo fabric flat, considers her collection of threads, chooses one. Sitting alone in the empty workroom, Fannie is both small and gloriously bright: her hair is a golden glow; her face belongs to a porcelain doll. The supervisor despises her all the more on account of that splinter of her soul which cannot help but admire the younger woman's dedication, her grace, her unbreakable composure. She has not noticed the red-raw dent at her fingertips, the painful splits in the skin around her fingernails.

'Getting a head start, Fannie?' she says. The girl has been arriving earlier and earlier – pilfering the sleekest runs of fabric, no doubt. The supervisor's words echo in the cavernous room. Fannie does not flinch, as many a disturbed person might. She would not permit herself such weakness, and the supervisor knows it.

'Yes,' Fannie nods. Her voice never alters; always her responses are delivered in the same soft alto. But this morning, she is exhausted – she had not slept a blink last night for worrying about the increasing cost of her daughter's medicine – and the supervisor's words cause her jaw to clench.

'I don't imagine the mayor will visit today,' the supervisor continues, her tone clipped, her feet deliberately heavy over the floorboards. Fannie feels the repeated thud low in her empty stomach. 'There'll be no one to impress.'

'All the same, I might aim to impress myself.' Fannie is not being glib. The answer is truthful. In everything now, she aims for fineness. But ordinarily, she wouldn't voice the thought. At the factory, she has learnt to be quiet, tolerant, unresponsive. 'There is nobility to be found in any job done well, don't you agree?'

Fannie lifts her head to meet the supervisor's eyes and finds them narrowed into blackness. Were she not so hateful, Fannie might tell her that her irises are the most unusual shade of caramel brown, and that her black hair gleams, and that if she should choose to frown a good deal less, she might be quite beautiful. Fannie bows her head again. She does not want to continue this conversation. It will only prove petty and circuitous, as conversations inside the factory walls ever do.

'Any job?' The supervisor's cheeks grow gaunt. 'Even the one them ladies of the night do?'

Fannie uses the last scraps of her energy to summon a smile. The supervisor expects her to retrace her words now, to stumble. But Fannie will not falter at being goaded today.

'Oh, yes,' she replies. 'Even those ladies. After all, they must develop their expertise, mustn't they? And practise. To pretend at pleasure hour after hour, well, I'd imagine it must be exhausting.'

Fannie can hardly believe what she has uttered. The words do not sound like her own, and she knows nothing of those unfortunate ladies except for what she glimpses on her walks, but she suspects that the supervisor will think the sentiment unseemly and so could not resist voicing it. The supervisor has extolled the virtues of *making one's way respectably and morally* in a far louder voice since she and the foreman ceased exchanging pleasant words. And indeed, she seems to wane at Fannie's reply. Throwing off her coat, she flusters across to the line of hooks, and fidgets there until the factory doors creak open again and five or six bonneted figures titter inside.

By mid-afternoon, the girls are sniggering into their garments at the frequency with which Fannie checks the clock, their hatred stirred up by the rankled supervisor.

'You haven't got a fellow waiting, have you, Fannie?' croons the worker to her immediate right. 'Finally?'

'Tick-tock, tick-tock,' says another. 'She'll need to persuade *someone* into her bed before she finds herself in the knacker's yard. You're not getting any younger, Fannie.'

'She'll be as wrinkled as her skirts before very long.'

They laugh as one, effecting the cackles of stage witches. The supervisor has long encouraged them in their teasing, but today it contains more venom. Fannie merely raises her chin against it. She is aware, naturally, that this only increases their spiteful urges, but her other option is to lower her head, and that she will not countenance.

'Have you seen, too, how she keeps checking her pocket?' At this, Fannie betrays her own promise and meets the glinting eye of the girl who has spoken. She is small-chinned and vapid. Her thin nose bears a hump at its bridge, as if broken and never properly healed. 'Ooh, I think I've hit a nerve!' the girl squeals, bumping the shoulder of the supervisor, who she sits close beside. Fannie feels her ears burning and inwardly curses her fair complexion. 'I only have, too,' the girl continues.

'She was fussing with a letter this morning,' joins in a broader girl, with smiling cheeks and a powerful bust.

'Let us see what it says, then, Fannie,' someone crows, making a grab for her pocket.

They are all gabbling at once now, discarding their garments and needles to close around Fannie. She quickly loses track of who is speaking, but she does not blanch as they form a tight circle and begin, like a cluck of chickens, to peck. They have never gone this far before. She should have stayed silent instead of sniping back at the supervisor. But Fannie is tired of silence. Tired of clamping her lips tight around the retorts she ought always to have shot at these women. Tired of endless days and sleepless nights. Tired of longing for the moment when she can return to the inn with a pocketful of coins and open her arms to her shining daughter. She sits erect, her hand clamped over her pocket. Soon, fingers are pinching at the skin of her arms, tearing at the neck of her blouse, pulling the pins from her hair. Strands of hair rip free; her blouse discharges a button. She feels as though flaming match heads are being stubbed out on her scalp, her shoulders, her arms.

When her hand is finally prised loose and her letter stolen, she leaps up and hurls herself at the girl who has taken it, hissing and scratching for all her worth. She does not look up until she has her hands clamped at the thief's collarbone. She sees then that it is the supervisor who holds her letter. For a moment, they all freeze.

'Please,' Fannie gasps. 'It's nothing. It's private.'

The supervisor smirks, then kicks Fannie square in the stomach. 'We'll see, shall we?' she crows, as Fannie stumbles backwards and her arms are grasped by two other girls, who hold her still while the supervisor turns, places one sturdy boot on the bench, and steps up onto the table. Dusty winter light endeavours through the high windows and descends at a frail diagonal. Caught in its blurred shaft, the supervisor is a looming shadow.

Fannie, breathing through the pain at her middle, looks past her into the rafters, blackened by countless old fires and pocked by the weight of moisture gathering in the smut and grime. They are hung with cobwebs. In one corner, a pair of common house martins nest: flits of blue, brown and white feather; echoing, spectral chirps.

The supervisor makes a show of clearing her throat.

'Dear Fannie,' she reads. The other girls stand captivated, heads tilted back, lips slightly parted. The two, who hold Fannie still, grip her tighter. 'I'm sorry to say that the money you send just isn't enough. If you cannot find more, our arrangement will have to be brought immediately to an end. Caring folk, we are, but charity we are not. We have our own to feed.'

The supervisor breaks off, peers over the top of the letter at Fannie.

'And what's this then?' she asks.

Fear thrums through Fannie like a fever. Sweat orbs above her upper lip, rolls between her breasts.

'You're not paying for someone to be cared for, are you, Fannie? You're not... hiding a child, perhaps, are you?'

The deliberation with which she delivers the words persuades Fannie that the supervisor knew everything before she ever had sight of the letter. That lad on the steps earlier – was he in league with her? Fannie slumps onto her knees. What does it matter now? The supervisor will tell the foreman, and the foreman will have his excuse to throw another woman on the mercy of the streets, and she has no idea how she will buy her daughter's medicine without this job.

'I...' she begins, but there are no words to fit her fear. It mutes her.

'Oh, Fannie. Your tongue wasn't so slow this morning. Come, we're all waiting to hear your great secret.'

The supervisor steps back down onto the bench and thence onto the floor. She lowers her face towards Fannie's until Fannie can feel the heat of her nose-tip against her own. She continues in a stage whisper, 'Is there a child, Fannie? Because you know the rules, I'm sure, about unmarried mothers in this factory, don't you? There have always been strict rules here, about unmarried mothers.'

Fannie wants to close her mouth, so that she might shut out the taste of the supervisor's stale threats, but she is panting too heavily. Her chest heaves. The supervisor's eyes are round with feigned innocence. Murmurings move amongst the gathered girls.

'Who'd have thought...'

'And her maintaining that superior attitude when all the time...'

'Thinking herself better than the rest of us....'

Fannie moves to snatch back the letter, and manages to break free of the fingers pinched around her arms, but the supervisor dodges her. Fury surges through her every nerve then, and she doesn't even think about what comes next. Her muscles act independently of her mind. Her right arm flies out to her side, she swings from her shoulder, and with all the might she can muster, she slaps the supervisor hard across her face.

The crack of it is repeated by the scowling rafters. It is accompanied by the collective gasp of the girls. And then, as anticipated, by the boot-steps of the foreman as he storms across the factory floor. Fannie feels the boards shifting beneath her feet, the wood springing with each thump. But she does not shrink. She will not. She finds the supervisor's eyes and, holding them, opens her mouth to a smile. However frightening this is, there is freedom in it, too. Fannie knows now that she will walk out of this factory today and never return, and the thought sends her soaring from terror to euphoria and back again.

'Don't imagine I didn't see that, you fucking madam.' He stops before her and jabs his fists against his hips. 'Collect your things and get out!'

Fannie spins on her heel. 'But...'

The foreman menaces her from a height of near six and a half feet. He is three times as wide as she. She cannot fight him.

And no, she finds, she will not beg him. She swallows the *please* which had been threatening her throat. The room is made suddenly hot by so many bodies: their gossiping, their belching, their yawns, their perspiration, their coughs. Fannie can feel droplets of these people wetting her skin, and she cannot stand it a second longer. She stops to retrieve nothing. She owns nothing of worth but her choices, and moment by moment she is growing more convinced that something new lies ahead – a future she might take control of. A future in which she might mother her daughter again.

Without another word, she strides towards the door at the furthest end of the workroom. Beneath its heavy wood, a pale crack of daylight shows her the way. She does not glance back.

Rebecca F John's fiction includes a short-story collection, *Clown's Shoes* (Parthian), a short story, 'The Glove Maker's Numbers', that was shortlisted for the Sunday Times EFG Short Story Award, and a novel, the Costa award-nominated *The Haunting of Henry Twist* (Serpent's Tail). She publishes her first children's book with Firefly next year. This fiction preview is from *Fannie* (a feminist reimagining of the story of Fantine from *Les Misérables*), published by Honno on 26 February, the birthday of Victor Hugo.